Living Life, Facing Death
A Better Way of Living and Dying

Paul W. Murphey

To Steve and Sandy,
Knowing you is such
a pleasure. May your life
be ever more satisfying
and complete.
Paul
Paul W. Murphey

LUCAS PARK BOOKS

ST. LOUIS, MISSOURI

Paperback: ISBN 978-1-60350-019-7
Hardcover: ISBN 978-1-60350-020-3

Published by Lucas Park Books
www.lucasparkbooks.com

Printed in the United States of America

Contents

Preface

Death fascinates us! It baffles, bewilders, bothers, mystifies, perplexes, and intrigues us today, just as it has since the earliest human beings became aware of it. It has been a recurrent theme in all historical periods and places. Concern with death in our society has reached enormous proportions. Books, articles, movies, videos, and television programs dealing with aspects of the mystery of death flow incessantly. A recent Google search for "death and dying" (07/04/2011) produced 14,700,000 references.

Tuesdays with Morrie by Mitch Albom stayed on the *New York Times* best seller list for about five years. Tens of thousands read and discussed it. An award winning television movie was made from it and attracted an even wider audience. *The Last Lecture* by Randy Pausch, Carnegie Mellon University Professor, drew a phenomenal number of viewers to its appearance on You Tube and reached thousands of others who read it in book form (Hyperion, 2008).

For much of the 20th century death and sex were not topics for polite conversation.[1]

That changed when Jessica Mitford's *American Way of Death* irreverently broke the silence and began a new conversation. Her book concentrated on the lucrative funeral and burial customs and practices carefully orchestrated to cover-over the reality of death in our society. At the time she wrote the funeral industry made up a sizeable segment of the economy. A bit earlier than that, Evelyn Waugh satirically focused on the celebrity status of Forest Lawn Cemetery in California. His novel, *The Loved One,* was made into a movie which made his sardonic humor more widely known.[2] Cooperatives like People's Memorial Association and The Neptune Society have done much to lower the cost of disposal of the body, make cremation more accessible, and provide a channel for organ donation following death. In the past few years there has been a questioning of the appropriateness of American funeral practices and the development of more economical rites and "green funeral practices".[3]

The movie, *The Bucket List,* starring two celebrated actors took the old saying of "kicking the bucket" as a euphemism for dying to new heights. The HBO series *Six Feet Under,* about the trials and tribulations of a family running a Los Angeles Funeral Home, drew devoted viewers for five seasons. Death is courted in the reckless abandon of automotive thrills, the sensationalism of reality TV shows, and the glorification of war and death in combat.[4] Magazines, newspapers, and computer blogs sometimes treat death inanely and at other times quite seriously.

With all this exposure, why then another book on death? Quite simply, because death is probably the most insistent human mystery compelling us to probe our existence and life's meaning. Like all great themes of our human experience the vantage points and perspectives change not only with the times but with the experiences of both writers and readers. It is hoped that this book will in both a personal and professional way have something worthwhile to say to anyone seriously wanting to grapple with the meaning of death and ways of coping with it. The earlier parts of it will probably be better understood by someone with a strong theological background, whether from seminary or graduate school or from undergraduate liberal arts studies. Anyone wishing to acquire the knowledge of a college course on death and dying could hardly do better than to study *The Last Dance: Encountering Death and Dying* by Lynne Ann DeSpelder and Albert Lee Strickland. This inclusive interdisciplinary approach is now in its ninth edition testifying to its popularity and usefulness as a college textbook. One of the finest contributions to raising consciousness about facing death with integrity was the PBS four-part series "On Our Own Terms" hosted by Bill Moyers. It aired first in 2000 and was supported by a superb website with a variety of rich resources.

You may find it more interesting to read Chapter 7 first and then come back and start from the beginning. That would give you a feel for the human dimension of the treatment of death which is developed in the book. Progressively the chapters explore the mystery of death first as an intensely personal and universally relevant human event. Death is then explored as an event in which fact is inseparably bound up with meaning or interpretation. Death is a sacred or religious issue in the deepest sense of the word. The mystery of death is viewed from perspectives of the Old and New Testaments. The Christian heritage, based on the biblical experience, is a historical response to the human condition which adds to our understanding. The insights and treatments of other religions and philosophies make their own valuable contributions to better understanding of death and dying. Pertinent theological treatments have been selected and emphasized for what they have to offer. These chapters prepare for the last chapters in which we look at the vital dimensions of coping with death—our own and other persons—and look at the unique place of hospice in coping with death.

As a person who loves life and savors its joys death has fascinated me for most of my long life. I firmly believe existentially that we are not able to truly live our human life until we have taken death seriously. It has hounded me as a teacher of philosophy and religion seeking insight into the most profound mysteries of our existence. My teaching career in history, philosophy, religion, and interdisciplinary humanities would have been severely impoverished if awareness, depictions, observances, and considerations of death had been denied. Ministry with and to others in the occasion of death both in civilian pastoral settings and as a U.S. Navy chaplain made an indelible mark. In the latter part of my life nothing has caused me to live my life more mindful of facing death than my deep involvement with hospice. Traveling the last stage of the journey with people I have come to love, respect, and admire has enriched my life and thought far beyond my ability to put into words. Nevertheless, I am deeply grateful to all those persons along life's journey who have permitted me the privilege of sharing in their lives, their thoughts and feelings, and their deaths. I hope what follows in this book will be a way of expanding those precious human encounters.

I am indebted to more persons than I can mention for what I have written. Students in courses or seminars I taught on death and dying provided lively interchange and insight. Colleagues were helpful in making me aware of resources and the need to more adequately express what I was trying to say. Three persons above all others deserve more gratitude than these simple words convey. David Gunderlach former fellow Chaplain on USS MIDWAY and a stimulating Mensa protagonist critically examined the first draft and encouraged me to make it better. Laurie Cook Liberty whose friendship I have enjoyed over the years as a student, a colleague, and a deeply caring friend lovingly made improvements in style as well as urged me to bring greater consistency in blending scholarly accuracy with personal experience. No one could have done more than Dr. Loren Logsdon whom I have known for over fifty years since our earliest teaching days at Eureka College. Loren continues to enlighten students there and gave me the same meticulous guidance on technical matters of documentation he lavishes on all his students. In spite of his full teaching load he found time to read the manuscript line by line and make suggestions for revision. Of course, any inadequacies are mine alone; any positive benefits derived from reading this work come from the generosity, encouragement, and kindness of others.

I cannot thank Richard Duchaine enough for giving his kind permission for me to include the role hospice played in the life and death of his deceased wife Mary Elizabeth (Beth), former Executive Director, Hospice of Kitsap County. Sharing her story demonstrates as nothing else could how hospice can truly be a better way of living and dying. I owe John Wicks and his daughter Jocelyn a deep debt of gratitude for letting me share something about Pat, former Volunteer Coordinator of Hospice of Kitsap County who had such a positive influence on so many persons involved with hospice. That same debt of gratitude is owed to all the nameless others who also have graciously given their permission to share the often poignant and always helpful stories of those so dear to them.

My heartfelt thanks to Gail Stobaugh of Lucas Park Books who made my dreams a reality and did it with such grace and skill and to Lynne Condellone, graphic artist, who made the book come alive from front to back. As I conclude this work, I am painfully aware of the incredible number of works on death and dying which are not mentioned even in the body of the work, the notes, and the list of resources at the end. But, like life and death themselves, there is in writing about them no final beginning nor end, only a place to start and a time to stop.

[1] See William May, "The Conspiracy of Silence," (1962) pp. 52–56 and Geoffrey Gorer, "The Pornography of Death," (1960) pp. 402–407 for an explanation of the reticence concerning death. Woody Allen has treated sex and death almost as twin topics in several of his popular movies, especially *Love and Death* (1975). Ingmar Bergman became a cult figure with the solemnity of his treatment of death and angst.

[2] The screenplay for the movie which came out in 1965 was based on Waugh's novel as well as on Jessica Mitford, *The American Way of Death* (1963). Another delightful movie celebrating life utilizing macabre humor is the film *Harold and Maude (DVD 2000)*. American funeral solemnity and contemporary avoidance of the reality of death is satirized and several other sensitive topics are explored with levity.

[3] See Rachel Pritchett, "Going Green into the Ground", (2009) pp. A1 and A4.

[4] See Toynbee, "Death in War," (1969) pp. 145-152.

Chapter 1

Death—A Human Event

Death—a universally unavoidable human event

Can you remember the first time you faced death? Was it when you found a lifeless bird and vainly tried to flap its wings or give it back its song? Was it when your dog lay mangled and unresponsive to your sobs, the victim of her running into an oncoming automobile? Was it when your grandfather "passed away" and the seldom-seen relatives with alternating whispers and silence sent you away?

We face death differently but death meets most of us early in life. For some the specter of death hangs as a foreboding presence. For others it comes swiftly without warning. Inevitably it comes early or late, swiftly or slowly, naturally or accidentally. It meets us and is then never far from us until eventually we come to face our own death.

When did you last face death? Was it when you sat with a few others in a funeral chapel or stood at a graveside while someone performed "last rites"? Was it when you watched anxiously with friends whose son's senseless accident culminated in death? Was it when someone of your own family whose life had been intimately shared whose very flesh was your flesh and blood your blood was now still and silent?

We face death as an unavoidable fact of our human existence. It may be forestalled, prolonged, postponed, or delayed.

1

Nevertheless it comes. Death is a stubborn human event rather than an academic or intellectual issue. Those who write or think perceptively about death know that the fact of death is not simply an objective event. They know as the simplest person knows that death will not leave us alone and untouched. We like they will die. There is no question that we will die; it is only a matter of when and how and why?

Death has many faces. It is therefore quite legitimate today that concern for the death of cities, lakes, streams, rivers, seashores should be explored in depth so that means may be found for preventing such waste and destruction. Pollution is a slow strangulation of the windpipe by which communities are sustained. Ecological death is an ominous threat which must be taken seriously.

Crucial for an intellectual approach to death is personalized death in a depersonalizing world. Many have written of the fate of men and women in the modern world as one of persistent dehumanization.[1] Technology which has advanced human beings so incredibly toward the stars can as easily blast us to dust or grind us into insignificance. What irony there is that the creations we have fashioned in an attempt to find our place in the sun after the sun displaced the earth as the center of the universe should now poise us on the verge of cosmic disaster from the sun's energy. What irony that the tools we fabricated to extend our power now render us powerless. How absurd that we continue to build weapons capable of contaminating the atmosphere to such an extent that human life itself could be completely obliterated.

Even if we start with death as an academic problem sooner or later we are faced with our own mortality: "An open grave at once reminds us that we are not simply concerned with a matter of academic discussion." (Cullman 51) We may become sufficiently desensitized to the suffering, tragedy, loss, or death of others so that their death is merely an objective fact. We can then pass quickly over their obituary on our way to the sports, society, or financial section of the newspaper. At some point, however, we become aware of our own mortality and the inevitability of our own death. For some persons with heightened empathy the death of others has all the qualities of a human, rather than an intellectual event. They like John Donne have discovered that since "no man is an island complete to itself" the tolling of the bell is for them. To die is the last human event. In that profound awareness beyond reasoned analysis death is a universal, inevitable human event without exception.

We face many issues which have only limited application. Every segment of society and each specialization has its own jargon for treating its basic concerns. Communication is often difficult because of one group's ignorance of another's methodology and nomenclature. Much in life is restricted or off-limits either because we do not have the credentials to gain admission or the understanding to comprehend the ramifications of what is being denied us. But death is not such an area. It like birth is a universal and inevitable human experience. As Edmund Volkart and Stanley Michael have observed:

> In the first place, human death is a universal and re-curring event. Every culture has its own values, ideas, beliefs, and practices concerning it. An individual learns the orientation of his culture toward death; and thus when he is faced with bereavement, one factor involved is his conception of the meaning of death. In this connection many, if not most societies throughout the world do not regard the event of death as being an inevitable fact of life; rather, it is often construed as being the result of an accident, of negligence, or of malice on the part of magicians or sorcerers. Similarly, the cultural orientation of many peoples toward death is that it represents a gain for the deceased, an improvement in his prospects and status, and that mourning for his loss of life is inappropriate. These are in marked contrast to our own prevailing beliefs, for with us death is inevitable and the fate of the deceased is by no means as clear and as certain as it may once have been in the Christian tradition. (272–273)

Death is the distant border every living person must cross just as birth was the boundary over which we entered life.

We all enter life by the same narrow passage. We all leave by another narrow passage. Both are big enough for only one at a time to enter or leave. The customs and ceremonies accompanying these primal experiences are culturally diffuse but their centrality is universal. Provisions for dealing with the fact of death are found in all cultures. At great personal and social sacrifice men and women have ventured to find some elixir, some fountain of youth, some city of gold which would guarantee them a way of refuting the universality and inevitability of their death. No such way has yet been found and very likely never will be. Sometimes our contemporary manifestation of this quest confuses means and ends making extravagant and unsupportable claims. Even valuable advances in medicine and medical technology cannot eliminate the mystery of death. They can indeed aid us with death's related dimensions—disease, aging, and dying—but not with the mystery of death itself. The word mystery has been deliberately chosen as a term which connotes that when we know all that we can know of something we then become acutely aware of how much we still do not know. This is poignantly true in our intimate personal relationships with one another. This concept of mystery is contrasted with that of the term problem. Problems can be solved; mysteries can only be experienced and known up to a point.[2] It seems to me that this is the essence of Socrates' ironic statement that he "knew nothing" in objecting to the claim that he was the wisest of all men. It was not that he literally knew nothing, but that what he did know left him unsettlingly aware of how much more there was to know. Albert Einstein, selected by *Time* as the greatest intellect of the 20th century, saw reality including truth much the same way. For him mystery was an essential element of our humanity especially as one tries to come to grips with the realities of the universe, "The most beautiful emotion we can experience is the mysterious. It is the fundamental emotion that stands at the cradle of all true art and science. He to whom this emotion is a stranger, who can no longer wonder and stand rapt in awe, is as good as dead, a snuffed-out candle."(Quoted in Isaacson 387)

Contemporary culture loses so much of that sense of mystery because it is so youth oriented. The growing number of aging persons has become an affront to our society's basic conviction that the real values in life belong to the youthful, robust, and active. Robert Fulton has made this pertinent observation:

> The aged, those most susceptible to death, seek in ever-increasing numbers to remove themselves to segregated retirement communities, there to await fate in the same manner as the leper once did. Death, like a noxious disease has become a taboo subject, and as such it is both the object of much disguise and denial as well of raucous and macabre humor. ("Death and Identity" 4)

Our failure to deal adequately with the problems of the aging in our society is not simply a matter of lack of competency or resources. That failure is rather a refusal to come to grips with our basic conviction that the only life worth living is the life of the young. Again, Robert Fulton speaks to the situation of our culture, "Modern America with its emphasis upon youth, health, sports cars, long vacations, and longevity has come to view death as an infringement upon the right to life and upon the pursuit of happiness." ("The Sacred and the Secular" 100)

Catherine Mayer has coined the word amortality for this refusal to prize any phase of life as worthwhile except perpetual youthfulness. As she says, "Amortals don't just dread extinction. They deny it". (53) As a culture we have oversold ourselves on the virtues of youthfulness and deprecated the qualities which come with aging. We have segmented life and cannot see death as belonging to it. Death and life are no longer two sides of the same coin but two separate and distinct realities. Our preoccupation with the present represented by our thirst for youthful aliveness leaves us with an inadequate sense of time as appropriate development or rounding out our existence culminating in death.

Youth is not seen as the midpoint in a full human life. It is instead the peak toward which all rush and from which few want to descend. In fantasizing youth we have romanticized old age and severed youth and age from one another. Is it any wonder that death has become the focus of so much of our popular culture?

Movies and television usually treat it with the illusion that no one really dies as a result of extreme violence. Though the hero is often mercilessly beaten or bloodied he returns next week or in the sequel to fight again. These manifestations of the American tradition do little to prepare us to cope with suffering, tragedy, and death.[3]

A notable exception to this was the television coverage of the death and burial of President John F. Kennedy traumatizing the nation for days in 1963. In that experience death was real. It had come to one for whom youthful vigor had not been sufficient armor. He had been incomprehensibly struck down in spite of his vigor. Somehow every man and woman saw in his death the awareness that he or she too must die. For some there was in that event the horrible suspicion that the culture itself was confronting its own premature death.

It may well be that we are better prepared because of the priorities of our culture to deal with such accidental death than we are to deal with natural death. In times like that the social adrenalin flows therapeutically to grapple with the requirements of doing what must be done because of the immediacy of the problem at hand. Its immediacy leaves little time for us to integrate the inevitability of death on a long term basis. Perhaps our technocratic, pragmatic, youth-oriented, crisis-poised culture leaves us with no appropriate means of integrating death and life in their usual courses.

Maybe only people who live close to the earth or the sea, who know the rhythm of planting and harvesting, or of coming and going, can see death as a part of life. Maybe our rapidly changing mechanization where a product is obsolete even before its computer designed model is complete leaves us with no categories for understanding and accepting the fact of how crucial an event death is. Maybe the only meaningful death will increasingly come to be either the accidental or the planned death. The accidental fits our perceptions of life where rapidity of change is life's measure. The real things are those that are constantly improved upon. Accidental death is seen as a universal probability.

What of planned death under the forms of euthanasia and suicide? It may well be that both of these which were prohibited in the past by religious sanctions will now be seen as somehow part of persons saving themselves. In a society which reduces the area of control any one of us may exercise euthanasia and suicide may be seen as defiant symbols of a person asserting control over his or her destiny.

Though both Oregon and Washington have legalized euthanasia some of the cautions expressed in the campaigns leading up to those enactments were expressed by Arnold Toynbee almost half a century ago. Toynbee cautioned against the decision to take one's life or precipitate one's death becoming merely an individual, independent matter:

> ...even if it were granted (and this issue is still a controversial one in the West) that suicide is a basic human right—at least for a human being to whom life has become a burden— there might be good grounds for holding that the exercise of this right should be subject to consideration and endorsement by responsible public authorities. Before giving their consent, the authorities ought to satisfy themselves that suicide is the patient's firm and well-considered choice, and that it is not the desperate whim of a mood of melancholia that might pass. Above all, they must be satisfied that the patient is not contemplating suicide under pressure from other people—and this is a contingency against which the public authorities would have to be on their guard; for anyone who is both old and incapacitated is inevitably a burden on society in general and on his own nearer relatives in particular; and, if he happens to be a man of property, his relatives might have a positive as well as a negative interest in his dying sooner rather than later. (158)

It may be that death's universality and inevitability will thus be reinterpreted. It may be that a culture fixated on action and whose members are heirs of Horatio Alger will take one of two routes—either we will feverishly seek to eliminate death, for example through such means as cryogenics, or block it completely out by hiding its presence as an obscenity.[4] In either case we would create an ever deepening chasm between youth and age. It is conceivable that we might even urge each man or woman to die his or her death as a final defiant act of taking their own life as an inalienable human right as Toynbee surmised. It may be that a third way is fast opening to us—talking death to death since so much is currently being written about it. It could become so much a rational or intellectual issue that it would lose its impact as a genuine human mystery.

The impossibility of exhaustively describing death

Many persons will possibly see the mystery as too obvious to be profound. Because it is so universal and inevitable there is sometimes the failure to realize that profundity lies in simplicity not in complex obscurity. Yet, there is nothing simple about the myriad attempts to either describe or define death. Even if a person deliberately contents himself with treating the problem descriptively avoiding any kind of normative issues he finds no easy task. The masks of death are as varied as the designs of nature and the creations of human imagination.

In many ways the favored mask is death in old age at the end of a long life. The Old Testament writers found such a death a natural experience. A person prayed for a long and fruitful life and peace at the last. To die of old age was to die a death akin to sleep after an exhausting but satisfying day. But not all death is the culmination of life fulfilled. Death in old age may be agonizing reflection on missed opportunities or life wasted. Maybe this is part of what is being expressed when someone says "old age is sometimes just hell", or "old age is not for sissies." Old age when the chance of any kind of meaningful life has vanished is but another face of death awaiting the dissolution of the body to catch up with the atrophying of mind and spirit. It is an experience akin to Moses standing on Mount Nebo viewing the promised-land. (Deuteronomy 34:1–4) All that one has worked his whole life for is now sadly beyond his grasp. He now sees that what he worked for all his life cannot and will not be accomplished. He must hand over the uncompleted tasks to someone else. The dreams have coalesced into the painful realities of the incompleteness of a human life. The face of death in old age may wear a bittersweet smile.

For others death may be release from suffering, agony, torture of body and spirit. It may wear the paraphernalia of tubes and bottles keeping the vital organic functions going and prolonging biological existence. Death may then come with little pain but also with little consciousness. A person then dies the death of the disease not his or her own death. What should have been personally his own death may have become impersonally institutionalized so that he becomes another corpse for the "organ recital" of the pathologist.

Death may wear the cruel face of the death of a youth or of a child fallen victim to some dread disease.[5] It may jar us momentarily as we consider some indiscriminate bombing in a Middle Eastern marketplace because of the act of a suicide bomber. Death may sneak up on us by way of a careless throwing of a rock or discharge from an "unloaded" gun, some accidental end coming from intended fun in the water or while racing excitedly. It may come as the result of a reckless or drunken or drugged driver who has abdicated his human responsibility. There is apparently no end to the way death may meet us.

Men and women often court death perhaps in an effort to prove the value of life. The risk contributes to the sense of being alive, of cheating death, of mastering one's fears or anxieties in a literal or figurative game of Russian roulette. Every time a person makes another leap from the plane or another lap around the race track there is the relief of being alive, of having made it. In the mid-20th century Evel Knievel became an American folk hero gathering enormous crowds and amassing tremendous fortunes as he cheated death by bold daring into which so many others entered vicariously. Symbolically men and women engage in thrill sports or diversions as a way of wrestling with the last enemy. The odds are great in high risk sports but the person who lives to tell it has won not just his life once again but the almost arrogant acclaim to have faced death and at least for that time conquered it.

Similarly men and women engage in hazardous occupations as a contest with death. A structural steel worker walks the narrow beam of the skyscraper under construction knowing that one loss of nerve, one misplaced step, one thoughtless leaning into the wind brings death. Miners go into the black hole of the earth as a descent into the grave each time with the hope and prayer of emerging as victors over the darkness and persistent threat to fragile life which can be snuffed out

unceremoniously. Jet fighter pilots fly their birds determined
that there will be no loss of nerve or disorientation or vertigo
and will land safely again with the proud acclamation of having
"really lived".

The military provides the most obvious array of death-ori-
ented occupations. Whatever death's form on land, at sea, or
in the air such occupations present men and women with the
necessity of risking life—their own or someone else's. They are
trained for the offensive pursuit of death whether in antiquated
anachronisms like bayonet drill or hand-to-hand combat or the
sophisticated electronics of piloting an unmanned drone from
half a world away. The mission is bound up with death. It is
easy to slip into a conviction that it is really only a matter of
"their deaths or ours". Even when considering the defensive
aspects of such occupations there is only a difference in degree
not in kind. A professional warrior must be prepared to ward
off any attack that threatens and nothing short of death is valor-
ous if that should be necessary. Such persons could hardly keep
their sanity if they constantly realized the actuality of the lethal
power of the weapons they tend thus they have been known
to paint on nuclear weapons the death notices of nameless
millions toward whom they might be aimed. They sometimes
engage in war games with the same intensity of professional
sports where valor, courage, and conquest, even obliteration
and annihilation are the goals obscuring the all too obvious difference that the object is not a trophy or a ring or maybe even
a lucrative bonus but death itself.

It is the appearance of such total death that hovers over
our age as of the earlier age of anxiety. It is still the age of
mass—masses of consumer goods to buy, of people crowding
one another, of roads clogged with people hurrying to places to
relax and escape the tensions of their mass existence. Not too
far away in the past we saw the mass murder of cities (Dres-
den, London, Tokyo, Hiroshima, Nagasaki) and well-known lo-
cales (Wounded Knee, My Lai, Darfur). Over the mass hangs
the sword of Damocles which with a few presses of vigilantly
guarded buttons could convert the planet into a whirling mau-
soleum.

The fact of death is inexhaustible to describe. Every age of human beings has had its dreaded death dealers. However the post-modern age has made us masters with mangling machines mutilating masses and posing for ourselves not just the problem of personal and individual death but the impersonal and mass death of mankind.[6]

The impossibility of conclusively defining death

If the multiplicity of forms death takes leaves us without a single sufficient description, will we be more able to find a conclusive definition? Sometimes the first step toward a solution to a problem is an adequate definition delineating the parameters.

We may begin with the simple statement that death is the opposite of life, or death is the cessation of life. Mervyn Shoor and Mary Speed state it this way, "Death, the total and permanent cessation of the vital functions of an organism, is the inevitable consequence of biological existence." (201) This does not advance us very far. Only if we have a clear concept of the nature of life will we be able to discern the nature of death. Strange as it may seem to those who take death seriously an exact definition of death acceptable to even so circumscribed an area as medicine is not universally agreed upon. Is it the moment when there is no longer a heart beat, pulse rate, or electro-static waves? Is it when organic functions reach an irreversible state? Keith Mant distinguishes between somatic death and molecular death: "Somatic death is the cessation of all vital functions such as the heart beat and respiration. Molecular or cellular death follows."(19) Is it when the oxygen supply to the brain reaches the point where irreversible damage is done to brain cells? While many doctors rely assuredly on the textbook definitions which settle the matter in terms of electro-magnetic impulses or involuntary reflexes, others in spite of their scientific erudition still stand baffled at the mystery of life and death.

While I was Duty Chaplain at a Naval Hospital aboard a Marine Corps Base I had two starkly different experiences that illustrate this question. Within twenty-four hours two patients were brought into the Emergency Room as a result of accidents. One was an eight year old boy who had been run over by an automobile. His head was opened by a lesion danger-ously close to exposing the brain and requiring delicate and intricate neurosurgery. A team of about twenty medical person-nel worked with him as pulse-rate and heart beat precariously slowed and life flickered. Repeatedly he appeared conscious then unconscious. Death seemed more in control than life. He lived. The other, a robust twenty-two year old male in perfect physical condition had been in a motorcycle accident and had a minor abrasion on his left knee and another on his chin. No other wounds were visible. X-rays disclosed no fracture of the skull. For hours the team worked to restore him to conscious-ness using every aid that bio-engineering and chemical infusion could provide. All of this was to no avail. His death brought a palpable sense of frustration, loss, and failure to the whole medical team. The lead physician, an extremely competent and conscientious man, responded later to my inquiries about these two patients. What had caused the death of one and not the other? "That's your department Chaplain. It is a mystery—God only knows. I honestly don't know and even the autopsy will probably not tell us."

Death is somewhat like another inconclusive problem in medical ethics—when does life begin? The answer to this leads to other questions, for example those about abortion. Is it at conception when sperm fertilizes the egg? Is it when the em-bryo takes fetal human form beginning to take the shape of male or female? Is it at some point in the gestation period when consciousness or pre-consciousness may be assumed to receive data which will affect the programming of post-natal experi-ences?

The answer to the question of a universally acceptable technical definition of life or of death is not conclusively avail-able to us. Yet the lack of such refined analytical information does not prevent us from knowing in practical or existential terms the presence of life or death.

Death is such a traumatic event that self-initiated move-ment is an impossibility. There is no longer the power of loco-motion, speech, or conscious communication. There is no lon-ger the power to respond voluntarily to external stimuli. The homeostasis which balanced integration and disintegration, growth and decline, vivification and deterioration now ceases. The wholeness of organic functions no longer has an integrative center. Whether we think of this on a model of electric circuits or self-restorative organisms, it is irreparable brokenness. In whatever way we define the fact of death it is human separation without the possibility of reunion.

The clinical and sterile terms used above are hardly the way a person speaks of death in intimate, personal human experiences. I shall never forget the tone, the inflections, the voice of the doctor who informed me over the telephone of the death of our first daughter. He callously pronounced, "She's gone bad you had better get up here." Just a short time before, I had gone home from the hospital to shower and change clothes before returning to be by my wife's bedside. It was as if the baby's life was no more to him than a piece of machinery which had broken down or a piece of overripe fruit that had rotted. Not dissimilarly, there was little comfort in the words of well-meaning church members whose motives were pure but who said such inane things as, "God wanted another flower for His garden."

Religion and the death event

Death may well be the central problem for religion. Herman Feifel stated this well: "Throughout man's history, the idea of death has posed the eternal mystery which is the core of our religious and philosophical systems of thought." (xiii) Religion may have arisen out of early human beings' attempts to come to grips with the baffling enigma of a once active companion now stilled to silence yielding no response. In the dumb loss of life some reply to plaintive wonder was necessary, some action to assuage grief, some thought to comfort amidst the perplexity.

A primary cultural function of religion is to provide means of accommodating human beings to the fact of death. Carl Jung goes so far as to say, "One might even say that the majority of these religions [the great religions of the world] are complicated systems of preparation for death...." (8) Taboos surrounded the dead and special qualifications were necessary to touch the defiling corpse. A period of contamination followed contact with the corpse and had to be purged with imprecations and ritual cleansing. A sense of the holy encircled the dead so that men and women were strangely attracted and repelled at the same time. Separated from the living they were often considered the bridge between this world and the next. The concept of the next world did not have to be highly refined. It was only essential that death be considered the passage out of this life into another world. That world might be one of gloom and deep darkness, or the abode of shades, or the sunny field of plenty, or even the "not land" of nothing and nowhere. (Kohler 113)

Judaism and Christianity both took death seriously. Christianity by the third or fourth century was moving in two directions relative to the twin human problems of sin and death. Western European Christianity under the formative influence of Tertullian, lawyer turned theologian, adopted a legalistic framework in which the major human problem with which Christianity had to deal was the problem of sin with its attendants—guilt, judgment, punishment, heaven, and hell. Consequently, the predominant theological thrust was toward men and women as sinners. Concepts of God stressed His power, justice, sovereignty, and judgment. Form followed function and the institutional church developed appropriate and elaborate rituals for dealing with the problem of sin. The mass was a perpetual repetition of Christ's sacrifice for man's sin. Death in the affirmation of the Apostle Paul was "the wages of sin".

Memento Mori, reminders of death, abounded in books such as *Death and the Ploughman* written by Johannes von Saaz in the 15th century.[7] The dance of death sought to ward off plagues and epidemics. No piece of art from that period depicted it better than Albrecht Durer's woodcut, "Knight, Death and the Devil". In that work the knight of faith rode off resisting the sinful temptations of the comfort of home, family, and friends to do battle with death and the devil. Death was the gruesome master come to pay the wages of sin to guilty men and women.

The orientation of western Christianity was not radically changed by the Protestant Reformation. The Erasmus/Luther debate on the freedom of the will was still a medieval foray into the territory of sin and death with salvation being primarily the gracious lifting of sinful human beings from the torments of hell awaiting them after death. The story continued much the same in America in the mid-18th century. Jonathan Edwards vividly expressed it: "sinners in the hands of an angry God" dangled precariously as by a spider's thread. This was the incessant theme as revival fires swept the colonies and then the newly founded nation in great religious awakenings. The growth of conservative Christianity usually carried with it an invigorated stress on the primacy of human sinfulness leading to death and everlasting punishment.

Two other major forces were at work. One was within Christianity and the other was a reaction against the prevailing religious world. Eastern Christianity in Asia Minor and Eastern Europe in the third and fourth centuries turned its focus to the ending of human life in death. Death, rather than sin, was its primary focus. Sin was not ignored but it was not Eastern Christianity's center of attention. Easter with elaborately moving rituals depicting resurrection from the dead was the focal point. Suffering and tragedy were inescapable elements of the human condition. Crucifixion the symbol of human suffering and tragedy was God's victory over death, humanity's last enemy, rather than the perpetual sacrifice of Christ on the cross for mankind's sin.

The other force gathering since the Renaissance in Western Europe was the secularization process. Secularization was not always anti-religious. Many Renaissance secularists were deeply religious men and women. Nevertheless it was a rejection of concentration on the after-life as of greater consequence than life in this world and with it a repudiation of man seen exclusively as sinner. Fascination with this world inevitably turned attention to man as creator, fabricator, and maker. Resistance from religiously sincere believers saw the elevation of human beings as a confirmation of man's incorrigibly sinful efforts to dethrone God. How astounding that men and women could believe for so long and so unquestionably that God could be God only by denigrating man and reducing him to nothing. Religious humanism of the Renaissance was an attempt to maintain the glory of God without sacrificing the dignity of man. Reasonable men and women sought to break the bonds of abject fear and crass superstition. How ironic that science which began as a way of valuing this world and maintaining the dignity of man now threatens both. Little wonder that men and women turned away from overwhelming consideration of death and sin to possibilities of life here and now and man's capabilities in such a world. The separation of death and life so sharply drawn in American culture has deep and understandable roots in the rise of science and humanism and the warfare of religion with these since the Renaissance.

Religion, even secularized civil religion, focuses on the death-event.[8] The burials following the assassinations of Abraham Lincoln, James Garfield, John and Robert Kennedy, and Martin Luther King, Jr. became religious events for the whole nation. Something deep within the society stirred men and women to ask about the meaning of life. Questions of our origin and destiny now were revitalized. One of religion's main functions is to provide appropriate means of response to these questions and ways of dealing meaningfully with the death-event.

Caring for one another facing death

Death—it can be said so easily. Yet sometimes we can hardly say it at all and resort to euphemisms: "she's passed on," "deceased", "he's no longer with us," "she was taken from us."[9] We can turn away from it with disdain, disgust, despair, desperation, disbelief, or dejection. Sometimes in frustration we cry out against the absurdity of human death and the futility of life in the face of death. We can also nonchalantly anesthetize our concern until we are later chagrined by our guilt at feeling deep inside, "I'm glad it wasn't me."

Living longer we deceive ourselves with the illusion that living longer means living better and living better means living forever. It is not surprising that Sigmund Freud emphasized what most perceptive persons discover from their own experiences that no man can consciously believe in his own death. As he famously said, "At bottom no one believes in his own death, or to put the same thing in another way in the unconscious every one of us is convinced of his own immortality."[10] It is not that we don't prepare for it in such ways as buying life insurance though for most of us there's the gnawing thought that whatever the amount it will not be enough to provide for our family as we would like.

Ministers and other care-givers stand so often in the place and time of death that they need no one to prove to them that death is an objective reality. They know it is not dependent upon what a person thinks or feels about it. Caring ministry is performed cognizant that death comes to the just and unjust alike, the noble and the ignoble, the saintly and the scurrilous, those prepared for its coming and those furtively fleeing it. Death has no special Christian, Jewish, Muslim or any other religious designation. Christians and Jews die just as do Muslims, Hindus, Buddhists, Scientologists and all other people of faith. Atheists, agnostics, disbelievers or whatever term they prefer for their stance also die. There is only one way out of this life and it is through the narrow passageway of death. Martin Luther expressed our existential plight: "Every man must do two things alone: he must do his own believing and his own dying."

Ministers, priests, rabbis, and all other religious care givers not only have to meet their own existential death but must function as religion's official interlocutors.[11] They are sometimes called upon to face the fact of death with those from different religious contexts than their own and even with those who profess no religious orientation whatsoever in facing death.

Meeting death is often the primary aspect of ministry exceeding even baptisms, weddings, confirmations and other religious ceremonies. I vividly remember my experience as an inexperienced undergraduate student pastor of a small church not far from Dallas, Texas. In the nine months I ministered there I had nine funerals. There were also several other situations pervading that little community marking it by death's omnipresence. Funerals often follow long periods of hospitalization or confinement at home or in a nursing home and a continued ministry to the bereaved or grief-stricken usually follows the terminal event.

Pastorally there is no such objective reality as death in the abstract. Every death is specific. It is George's, Bill's, Mary's, or Susan's death. The deceased is a person who once lived and who has died his/her own unique, individual, and un-substitutable death. There is probably no more emphatic point in Existentialist literature than this.[12] To approach each individual death as if it were but another in a series of pastoral duties is to sully the dignity of each person's life and to caricature the ministry performed in facing death. All men and women because they are human beings have a right to have their death taken seriously. This is not because they are Christians or persons with other religious commitments. Recognition of the life they live and the death they have died should not falsify who they were even to suit an uneasy ministerial conscience.

I grew up in the deep South at a time when death rituals were a recurrent experience even for a child. It came as a shock to me in my fifties when I moved to the Pacific Northwest to find it a daily occurrence to read in the morning newspaper at the end of an obituary, "at her request there will be no services." As human beings who hold to the dignity of life there is a need for some form of closure to acknowledge the life and mourn the death of another especially those close to us. It does not have to be a distinctively religious and formal service. All that is required is the recognition of the value of that person's life. That in itself is a religious act. Erick Lindemann said it well, "Even though it is true that how each person dies is determined by how he has lived, it would appear to be equally true that a dignified death proclaims the significance of all men." (186)

Every human being has an inalienable right to die with dignity, that is, to die the death fittingly appropriate to his or her life.[13] Occasionally through design, accident, or irony one man dies the death intended for another by being at the wrong place at the wrong time. Normally, however a person can only die his own death assuming he has lived his own life. This means that in his life he found authentic expression of his own interdependence as well as independence. For him life was responsible freedom and shared cooperation as well as faithful conformity and creative expression. To die one's own death is something other than dying the death of the disease one has contracted or the accident one has fallen victim to.

"Joseph Wittig once said that a biography should not begin with the birth of the person but rather with his death."[14] Death gives perspective for exploring the meaning of one's life consequently for all human existence. As Jacques Choron notes the question of the ultimate meaning of human existence "... may arise on various occasions, it is particularly likely to do so in connection with death." (160)

In the face of death men and women treat one another differently. There is not necessarily more kindness and compassion but there is often more honesty or integrity. Anticipating and accepting death provides a realistic vantage point for assessing the pursuits and directions of one's life. Ministry facing death seeks appropriate means of helping men and women encounter death not merely as a brute, objective fact, but as a moment of reality in which there is the confidence that fact and meaning, event and interpretation are inseparable. The truth we seek in this experience is the same as that which we seek in any genuine human endeavor—the flowing together of fact and interpretation. Without reliable fact the pursuit is doomed to failure. Equally important is the recognition that without integrative interpretation the facts are meaningless.

[1] Among the numerous sources treating this, Nicholas Berdyaev gives an impassioned assessment in his *The Fate of Man in the Modern World* (1935).

[2] See Gabriel Marcel, *The Mystery of Being* (1950) for a full discussion of this issue.

[3] See Paul Irion, *Funeral: Vestige or Value?* (1966) pp. 33, 36.

[4] Commenting on the death of actress Natasha Richardson as a result of a skiing accident, Richard Corliss referred to that as "her obscenely early death." in the March 30, 2009 issue of *Time* Magazine, page 22.

[5] Simon Yudkin, "Death and the Young" in *Man's Concern With Death,* (1969) pp. 46–55.

[6] See Hans Morgantheau, "Death in the Nuclear Age," (1967) pp. 69–77, and also Robert J. Lifton's study of the impact of effects of the atomic bomb on Hiroshima in *Death and Identity* (1965) pp. 8–42.

[7] Ernest K. Kirmann translated it into English and it was published in 1958 by the University of North Carolina Press.

[8] See Robert Bellah, "Civil Religion in America," *Daedelus* Winter, 1967. pp.1–21. This theme was developed more fully by Bellah and his associates in numerous articles and books which followed.

[9] See Toynbee, "Changing Attitudes Towards Death in the Modern Western World," (1968) "Present-day Americans, and other

present-day Westerners too in their degree, tend to say, instead of 'die,' 'pass on' or 'pass away,'" page 131.

[10] See Freud, *Thoughts for the times of War and Death* (1915) in his *Collected Papers*. New York: Basic Books, 1959, Vol. IV, page 305.

[11] There are two basic meanings of the term interlocutor: 1) intermediary—one who is in between, and 2) the minstrel's Mr. Interlocutor who serves as straight man to life's jokes.

[12] Among the almost limitless sources one might consult, a good place to begin would be Helmut Thielicke, *Death and Life* (1970).

[13] See Robert Fulton,, "Introduction to Part 2," *Death and Identity* (1965). Having talked about Americans' preferences and practices about where they die Fulton refers to Weisman and Hackett's concept of an 'appropriate death'...." page 82.

[14] Quoted in Helmut Thielicke, *Out of the Depths* (1962). page 78.

Chapter 2

Meanings of Death

Death as event

Death is not just a universal and inevitable fact. It is an event filled with meanings. These meanings include not only perspectives but realms of reality as well. Perspectives depend upon the condition and experiences of the person experiencing them. One of the basic axioms of the humanities is, "where you stand determines what you see". Think about it. If you are facing in one direction you cannot literally or physically see anything that is behind you in an opposite direction. It is not that there is nothing there. What is there may be seen only when you have put yourself in a position of seeing things from a different perspective. It is obvious that this is the case with physical sight. It is just as true figuratively. Realms unlike perspectives are of the very order of existence. They are ontological incorporating life and death. Perspectives depend upon the realms of reality in which the perceived events occur. Regardless of a person's perspective death is a fact.

Let us borrow a term from Martin Heidegger and refer to death as factical. In the factical realm death is material, physical biological and subject to the scrutiny of empirical verification. Our senses tell us whether something or someone is dead or alive. In this realm there may be disputes as to the precise moment of death or an adequate definition of death. There is no dispute that a man or woman dies biologically or physically. From the perspective of empirical verification biological death is an end to those dimensions of life referred to as ephemeral, spiritual, or historical. The fact of death belongs to men and women as natural biological beings. History rather than nature is the realm of the meanings of death. It is the order of reality in which human actions express a person's uniqueness or individuality. It is the realm of spiritual dimensions of human personality.

A human life is the flowing together of fact and meaning. The fact of death is validated by empirical observation; death's meaning is discernible in human history. Some form of meaning is authenticated even if the content of that meaning is not universally the same for all human beings. Each man or woman dies his or her death and that particular death has many meanings. As each person's life-history is different so the meanings of each person's death are different. The extent of the claim of death's meaningful universality and inevitability is that each human death carries with it some meaning or set of meanings. The claim is not that each death has the same explicit form, shape, or substance of those meanings either for that person or for others.

In his helpful book *How We Die: Reflections on Life's Final Chapter* Sherwin Nuland approaches death in terms of the effects various diseases and other causes of death have on a person's actual dying. He points out the differences these various contributors to death have on a person's ability to die his or her own death. At the heart of his work is the affirmation that each of us dies his or her own death:

> Every life is different from any that has gone before it, and so is every death. The uniqueness of each of us extends even to the way we die. Though most people know that various diseases carry us to our final hours by various paths, only very few comprehend the fullness of that endless multitude of ways by which the final forces of the human spirit can separate themselves from the body. Every one of death's diverse appearances is as distinctive as that singular face we each show the world during the days of life. Every man will yield up the ghost in a manner that the heavens have never

known before; every woman will go her final way in her own way. (3)

The two inseparable sides of the phenomenon death are necessary aspects of the death-event in much the same way that the crucifixion/resurrection is a single event for Christianity. In that particular death-event each aspect necessitates the other. Without the resurrection the crucifixion would be but another death by execution carrying no special importance for the salvation experience central to the Christian message. Without the crucifixion the resurrection loses its power of God's victory over death and the suffering and tragedy of human life it entails. Likewise, death as fact without meaning is but a blind and sometimes absurd final act awaiting performance by every man and woman. Death solely as meaning is but illusory fantasy, avoidance, or denial unless the fact is presupposed and taken seriously.

It is hard to accept the possibility of an absence of meaning for human death. We find it easier to accept absurdity rather than fulfillment or transfiguration as a form of meaning than to declare there is no meaning at all. Absurdity may be the meaning accompanying the fact of death for some persons. It is hardly the dominant meaning for all human beings.

In looking at death as fact and meaning a split between death as objective fact and death as subjective meaning is not intended or implied. Fact and meaning each has both an objective and subjective quality. However, there is a difference of emphasis. The emphasis of the factical is on objectivity while the emphasis of meaning is on subjectivity. My death is objectively mine for this particular material, physical, biological entity I have been throughout my life. When I die I die all over and that is a fact. No part of me continues to exist in its same form. All parts are disposed of equally by whatever burial rites are appropriate. Subjectively the meaning of this fact is dependent upon a configuration of lived experiences that make up the uniqueness of my life. The significance of this personal configuration is not subject to the same criteria of survival which are applied to the event of death as fact.

As all men and women experience death though the ways of death are not the same, so all human deaths carry meaning though the meanings vary with each human death. Human death is indisputably a factical/meaningful human event.

Meanings of death

What happens to us is important. Equally important is how it happens and how we perceive that happening. Our perceptions or pictures of reality are as significant for meaning as the reality they reflect. Truly, a person's perceptions of reality become the basis of his or her actions. Death is really a factual reality regardless of our perception of it. However, the meanings we attach to it affect us more deeply than the event itself. In the experience of death as in most other human experiences there is simply no such thing as a meaningless event. The meaning may be simple or complex, profound or superficial, revelatory or obscure but usually some multifaceted meaning is bound up with the event itself. These meanings are formed by many factors which are not all of the same order. There are meanings derived from our cultural heritage, meanings which come from the socialization we have received, meanings connected with temperament and personality, meanings accompanying our religious convictions or commitments and many other myriad meanings. It is appropriate to see the meaning of death as symbolic or metaphorical language. As Charles Wahl has observed, "We see ... that death is not only a state of physical cessation but it is also a complex symbol, the significance of which will vary from one person and culture to another, and which is also profoundly dependent upon the nature and vicissitudes of the developmental process." (64)

There is no conclusive list of meanings that exhausts the possibilities. One of the most basic meanings is to see it as a boundary situation before threatened annihilation. Death is what Paul Tillich, like Karl Jaspers, describes as a boundary situation. Human beings experience other boundary situations but death is primal. Here we are forced to the outer limits of our finite existence. Here the familiar territory is traversed and we are stopped by the barriers of the not yet experienced unknown. For some persons this provokes existential anxiety symbolized by the event of death. The temporal, physical fact raises the issue of an eternal and spiritual meaning. Death's boundary is not simply between living and dying it is between having lived meaningfully and the threat of the futility of such meaning. In ontological or metaphysical terms death is a question of being and not-being, of existence and extinction, of progression and annihilation. It is Hamlet's plaintive question: "to be or not to be". Such a situation grabs us at the deepest recesses of our being where we know existential anxiety—the irrational engulfing of our spirit with the nauseating possibility that in the vast immensity of reality beyond time and space we will not be. With this is the more sickening possibility that in the grand scheme of things our life has no basis for maintaining that there was a reason for our having ever been at all. Existential anxiety is not fear in that no object can be found which would allow us to deal effectively with it. We cannot flee it by deliberate effort. It is difficult to explain rationally. In fact, it is much like reading poetry—the poet depends on the reader having had a similar experience which her words bring to mind. Existential anxiety cannot be deliberately caused. If it comes at all to a person, it comes without preparation or warning and engulfs them in a sense of being lost in the blackness of infinite space without even the consciousness to make sense of it all. I can vividly remember how once in a while as a teenager I would be listening to music on the radio late at night after going to bed and the experience of existential anxiety would overwhelm me. It bore all the marks Tillich and others talk about including nausea and vertigo. I am grateful that it would go as quickly as it had come with no discernible after-effects.

There is the gnawing doubt that we will not be, that death is the end not just of relationships and familiar experiences but of what we call ourselves. For some there is anxiety because death is seen as a necessity at life's end. For others there is anxiety because that end may be not a completion of life but its extinction. We who were may be no more. For those persons neither the logically reasoned proofs for the immortality of the soul nor the myths of man's resurrection completely take away their anxiety. Ultimately we are unable to perceive death as annihilation. We view it as something happening to us not something destroying us totally. A person may imagine his own death—the experiences, rites and ceremonies connected with it—but he or she imagines it, creates the fantasies of self-transcendence whereby he or she becomes a spectator to the event in which he is the central participant. Anthony Flew explores this in a provocative article titled, "Can a Man Witness His Own Funeral?" Though we cannot imagine our death as annihilation, the nauseating possibility surges up unsolicited in the question "what if death is really the end after which there is no more now or ever?"

Death's meaning may be seen as fear. Fear unlike anxiety has a discernible object. We are afraid of heights, suffocation, failure, nuclear weapons, death; the list goes on and on. Our fear relative to death is often not so much of death as it is of dying. We fear the pain, suffering, sorrow of the actions leading up to the death-event. There is a fear which is not the fear of the process of dying but fear of death as the unknown. Life beyond death, "that undiscovered country from whose bourn no traveler returns," as Hamlet puts it, stands empty before us so that all our attempts to peer deeply into it leave us baffled and blind. There are no maps or guidebooks to the other side of death. Human beings have tried to provide such guidance in such resources as the *Egyptian Book of the Dead* or the *Tibetan Book of the Dead* as well as less widely known expressions in the folklore of most cultures. Every one of us ventures into the darkness of death without the benefit of the light of other men's knowledge. This does not stop us from speculating about the silence of death's unknown. Incredible explanations continue to be offered as they have been throughout history. One need only think of the fascination throughout the ages with reincarnation, psychic phenomena, near-death, and post-death experiences.

Another meaning for death is as a once-for-all event. In other areas of our life even if practice doesn't make perfect it equips us to handle more intelligently and confidently the situation the next time around. With death there is no next time.

From death's meaning as a once-for-all event, the sense of finality follows. (Choron 161) Usually if I make a mess of things I can do something to salvage part of what was intended. There are times when it is not possible to make things work out well when they have fallen in on top of us. With death there is the ring of finality much like the gavel of an auctioneer pointing to us and saying for all to hear "Sold!" Because it is final, we cannot say, "I'm sorry I made the wrong bid," or "I got carried away and didn't realize what I was doing." What is done is done. Nowhere is this more tragically seen than in those accidents of persons playfully pulling the trigger of a gun expecting only a click but instead seeing their friend fall dead before them. The shot cannot be called back. It hit its mark and the end of the matter of life is death. This was poignantly brought home to me in conducting the memorial service for a young sailor who according to his friends was simply playing Russian roulette for "a lark."

Death may also have the meaning of separation. The particular mode of separation dictates the meaning. Life may be expressed as a continual preparation for death. In that sense every separation, every absence, every journey is a little death readying us for what the poet Rilke called "the great death." Absence doesn't always make the heart grow fonder and many marriages, especially of military personnel, do not survive repeated separations or deployments. For many persons each departure is a little agonizing death. Kubler-Ross's helpful approach to analyzing what is happening to us as we experience death and dying is also applicable to divorce and other types of loss of long-term significant personal relationships. Yet the death-event is different. All the familiar supports of life such as family and friends, comfortable surroundings, and familiar accepted practices are given up for the un-experienced and unknown. Nicholas Berdyaev observed that when life is valued in terms of being together with someone you love the separation from them has the foreboding mood of a death in miniature. In his autobiography *Dream and Reality* Berdyaev remarked that the saddest thing to him was seeing two lovers on a park bench. In time they would recognize or admit that no matter how much they expected of their love it would never fulfill them completely nor would it have any ending but death.

It isn't that my own identity is severed and I am torn apart. It is rather that separation from those who give special qualities to my identity and who may even be my basic means of determining that identity takes away not just my happiness but my very well-being or personality. Death as separation from those whose relationship gives significance to my existence leaves me profoundly alone. Alienation is a particularly acute form of such separation in which even the proximity of physical presence cannot allay the agony of a spiritual chasm.

Alienation was a central theme at the midpoint of the 20th century in works of writers like Franz Kafka, Albert Camus, and Jean-Paul Sartre. Alienation leads inevitably to the problem of death as the breakup of meaningful community by the isolation of persons from one another. Nothing of significance is shared sufficiently to bridge the gap of our isolated existences.

Irreparable loss is akin to separation and affords another vantage point for discerning death's meaning. Death appears such an irreparable loss that we sometimes cry out, "what a waste." The loss is not experienced as temporary separation looking forward to reunion but as a painful awareness that there will be no return. There will be no further opportunities for fulfillment. No funeral service I have ever conducted brought such a bitter realization of this to me as the one I conducted for one of my uncles. In his younger life he had shown such promise and potential. But in his forties after several failed attempts at realizing those dreams he was found alone on the levee bank having died from acute alcohol poisoning. The incessant theme that would not let me go was, "what a waste."

Those who walk the lonesome road toward their death finally disappear out of sight. The loss is no longer a difference in degree, as in separation, but now a difference in kind. This is the burden of death.

Such awareness leads to another meaning when we realize it is not because of neglect or ineffectiveness but simply because of the structure of existence that the irreparable loss occurs. It now becomes apparent to us that death is an event over which we have no ultimate control. Death may be precipitated in more ways than we could list. In the end no matter how circumspectly or profligately a person lives death is waiting.

For some persons death has a meaning different than any of these. For them it is the means of equalizing the injustices and inequities of this life. The perversions of life lead to the punishments of death. Death for them is a control over and the culmination of a sinful life. Death is the price paid to live a human life. This may be the conclusion of the logic of original sin if one follows the Apostle Paul's dichotomy of human life marked by death as "the wages of sin" and the redeemed life as a new creation for indebted humanity which has been bought with a price greater than the debt of those wages. Christianity has chosen this meaning over most of the others for centuries.

A corollary of this is that because death is unpredictable and precarious it becomes the reminder to men and women of the contingency of their existence. It then becomes necessary to accept life as deriving from something other than itself. It is this human contingency in the face of death which is confronted in every theodicy from *Job* through John Milton's *Paradise Lost* to Archibald MacLeish's *J.B.* Atheistic existentialism speaks of our having been thrown into existence. Religious existentialism speaks of our having been sent into existence. Whether we speak of being "thrown" or "sent" into existence we acknowledge the givenness of life and with it the givenness of death. Death is something that happens to us even if we purposefully initiate it.

Religion and death's meanings

In the previous chapter we considered the relationship of religion to objective fact. In this one we are looking more closely at the way in which religion is involved in death's subjective side. Religion is the life men and women live to cope with death. This assertion about the nature of religion selectively concentrates on a single phenomenon. It is not meant to imply that religion has no other concerns. It does not say directly anything about the nature of the divine or the human. It is not so much a theological definition as a phenomenological observation. Religion is not the only means for coping with the mystery of death. Philosophy, science, the arts, psychology and a vast array of approaches find their advocates. Religion may be spoken of as ultimate concern having a permeating pervasiveness or as total commitment. It may also have the emphasis placed upon adherence to ritual, creed, or conduct. What is involved is avowal of the sacredness of human life and an affirmation of the reality of the holy.

Religion is broader than theology. Theology is the intellectualization of faith assertions considered worthy of acceptance. Religion is the universal dialectic between the divine and the human in time and space. It is historically and culturally molded and fashioned by the characteristics of particular religions. Religion is an abstraction which has ephemeral subsistence until it is concretized in a particular historic manifestation. Mankind is likewise a noble abstraction. White man, black man, primitive man, modern man are less abstract concepts though still abstractions. The man next door, this man, that man who is dying, that man who died yesterday transforms the abstraction into a reality I cannot evade.

In the sense that death happens to a man or woman and religion is the life he or she lives to cope with death it is then not an abstraction. It is a persistent means of encountering meaning in the event of death. Though it has often been assumed that religion has special meanings uniquely its own, this is not the case. The sacred has often been limited to certain or specific places, times, persons, rites, or beliefs. This fails to recognize religion's pervasiveness by making it simply another specialization contributing to the fragmentation of our human existence.

Religion is the integrative force giving cohesion to the segments of existence from the perspective of faith or the sacred, the divine, the holy. It does not provide us with another list of meanings considered inherently religious. It sees the meanings we have previously looked at with the possibility that they may, or may not, be religious. The religious nature of the meaning depends on the perspective of interpretation and not on some sacral quality in the meaning itself.

Existential anxiety and the threat of annihilation is significant from a religious perspective. Being religious does not alter the human situation in which one knows the nauseating question of "what if I die and there is nothing after that?" Religion is not committed to human invulnerability or immortality or ontological necessity in meeting death. Instead, it asks whether a human being facing his death and the threat of annihilation can trust in the meaningfulness of life affirming the glory of God and the dignity of man.

While it may be slight comfort to abandon hope of personal continuation of life after death it is not an irreligious act to do so. Anxiety may be met by intellectually establishing logical reasons for accepting a conclusion of annihilation. It also may be dealt with by affirming that it is inconceivable, at least for the person making the claim, that a God who makes his or her existence possible would annihilate it after so short a span. Life is seen as more than a flickering flame snuffed out by death. Anxiety does not necessitate a specific religious answer such as survival after death and a definite non-religious answer such as annihilation. Faith may contend that either answer may be religious or irreligious. The acceptance of the meaning as a sign of the sacred in the presence of life and death is a matter of faith. Faith is not blindly clinging to absurdities. It is quiet confidence that God is God in whom one can trust even in the face of the worst that may occur. It is conceivable that annihilation may not be the worst possibility in light of the lurid torments and tortures of eternal hells depicted in scenes from Hieronymous Bosch or the Buddhist Hell Scroll or seen in a visit to the Tiger Balm Gardens in Singapore or Hong Kong or in the well known pages of Dante's *Inferno*.

Annihilation is active negation but fear of the unknown is a phenomenon expressing a range of possibilities. It moves from collective agnosticism to conjecturing endlessly on the "what ifs" of a realm which cannot be subjected to verification by scientific/technological methods. It may even accept as real the placid speculations of "green pastures" as in Marc Connelly's play by that name which comically projects the known human predicament into the unknown situation beyond death. Or it may look off into the distance at Elysian Fields or Nirvana.

Personality growth requires venturing into new experiences which once they have been lived through give us confidence for approaching the next similar unknown.

Religion is living life relative to the unknown in such a way as to integrate natural fear into the equally natural awe and wonder at experiencing the new. Even those who have found the unknown beneficial and who approach it in an attitude of confident anticipation are not released completely from the fear of the unknown. Death may still assume a meaning of something unknown, but it can be faced honestly with hope. As they have repeatedly encountered the unknown without it destroying them, so they face the unknown of death with similar confidence. It may be expressed by saying, "before I came into this world it was unknown to me, but it has turned out all right; so as I leave this world I trust that whatever unknown world awaits me will be even better than this one." On the other hand, persons whose fears find no rest or resolution know the horror of the unknown, not just in the actual experience but innumerably in those ceaseless anticipations which magnify it. As Shakespeare wisely observes in *Julius Caesar,*

> Cowards die many times before their deaths;
> The valiant never taste of death but once.
> Of all the wonders that I yet have heard,
> It seems to me most strange that men should fear;
> Seeing that death, a necessary end,
> Will come when it will come. (Act II, scene ii)

Religion acknowledges the unknown realm of death without being terrorized by it. When a person looks at the meaning of death as fear of the unknown from a religious perspective, he or she assumes a difference in degree to similar experiences which all through life have called forth a religious stance.

When we come to the meaning of death in terms of its once-for-allness, it is no longer a difference in degree but in kind. There is nothing to compare it to since with the exception of birth it is the one event which is universally once-for-all. Traditionally we have taken an attitude of once-for-allness toward many human events. Marriage is perhaps the best example. Even if marriage is not severed by divorce or separation the death of one of the partners often leads to remarriage. There is indeed a unique quality to many human experiences, perhaps even to all of them, so that they we can never repeat or duplicate them in an exact manner. But, in talking about death we are talking about a once-for-all experience where one ventures forth with the certainty that he will not be able to learn from it so as to do it better the next time. Religion is supportive of a man or woman encountering such an event. He or she faces death with hope derived from the faithfulness of the past and the loving fulfillment of the present. This once-for-allness poses perhaps as great a problem for contemporary Americans as any other meaning. Our society values the ability to do more and better things, to build bigger and finer products. Death is a challenge not just to life but to the philosophy of life by which we live. Religion is charged with assisting men and women in such a cultural setting to accept the legitimacy of a once-for-all event which provokes reflection upon the legitimacy of devotion in such a situation.

Akin to death's once-for-allness but with different emphases is the meaning of finality. Once-for-allness expresses our inability to try again so as to do something better the next time to perfect the process. Finality is cessation, a stopping, an emphatic assertion that that is all—there isn't any more. The final act in the human drama having been played out, death is the curtain which closes transporting the audience back from illusion to reality. The passage is too narrow to turn around and start again. Like the final exam it indicates the course is over. It is this matter of finality which poses the greatest threat to the element of hope from a religious perspective. The evidence may be persuasive that an inauthentic life has now ended, that the person never found himself or worse he destroyed not only his own life but other lives as well. Jacques Choron phrases it well, "It would seem, then, that it is not so much the fact of having to die in itself as the regret of not having 'lived' or of having wasted one's life, or of having made a 'mess' of it, that is the main cause of their mortal distress." (164)

Death, the temporal event, has traditionally carried eternal consequences. It has been the closing of the account, the sealing of one's fate. If the religious perspective is based on the quality of an individual's life and that life gives inadequate signs of validation then hope turns to despair. When the religious perspective is not limited to this finite and temporal span, eternity is not so much quantitative as qualitative. The basis of life is then on the nature of the Life-Giver. Finality though taken seriously is not taken ultimately. This response may move in any of several directions including reincarnation, spiritualism, or universalism. It may be seen as a progression of lives on different planes of existence conceived as an educational progress toward perfection. This last possibility I first learned from studying with Nels F.S. Ferre who spoke succinctly of it: "We say only that in the light of eternity as infinite duration there is endless opportunity for change. Time is thus the presupposition for the pedagogical process." (89)

The meaning of separation is dependent upon the circumstances or context of the persons involved. Death usually carries a connotation of negation. It may not necessarily have that meaning when seen as separation. If a person has suffered long or intensively and there is no prospect of recovery, then death may be experienced as a longed-for separation from that acute pain. If a person has already been cut off from meaningful or fulfilling relationships with others and lives in alienation from them, death may be the consummation of isolation. Alzheimer's is the cruelest of modern illnesses which calls into question all that we have maintained about human identity in terms of reason as Descartes did with his famous *cogito ergo sum* (I think therefore I am). If a person is defined as one who reasons and that capacity has been lost or so greatly diminished as to appear to have been lost, is the person who eventually dies the person who previously lived a meaningful life? Separation may be the painful forced severance from persons who have added meaning to that life.

It may be a setting aside of work unfinished or dreams yet unrealized. Death as separation is broader in possibilities of meaning than any of the meanings we have looked at thus far. It finds a religious response in the perceptiveness of persons sensing the meaning of the event as they respond in a genuinely human fashion. In discernment of what separation means to the dying person and in appropriate response to him or her, the divine presence may give to both of them a clearer expression of their humanity. Separation may become the occasion for hope for reunion in a realm where such separations are no longer necessary. At the least it may lead to the affirmation with Alfred Lord Tennyson that "'tis better to have loved and lost than never to have loved at all." (*In Memoriam*) It may also take the form of memorials of gratitude for the contributions of the deceased person's life.

The separation of death as irreparable loss is a particularly bitter form of separation. Here nothing is able to take the place of the one who dies. Loss is expressed as bereavement. Edmund Volkart and Stanley Michael express it this way: "In American culture, it is difficult to consider the social role of the bereaved person in other than very general terms, but it appears to center around ideas of loss and the desirability of expressing that loss and grief. The language makes 'bereavement' and 'loss' interchangeable terms." (288)

Life will go on without the one who dies, but involvement has been so extensive and intensive as to leave an emptiness which can only be endured and never filled. No amount of diversion or attempted concealment is adequate for assuaging the piquancy of such an experience. Death is the destroyer laying life waste by proclaiming human achievements and attachments absurd if not futile. Religion confronts such a meaning with the faith-affirmation that life is not an absurdity but a meaningful process. Life may pose problems for which there are no solutions since the problem is never eradicated, but at least the problem is a significant one. Confronting the dimension of death as loss from a religious perspective lets one see other aspects of the problem. Suppose there were no death but old age and disease continued so that men and women grew interminably weaker but could not die. Or consider the population problem if all persons who have ever been born were still alive.

The meaning of death as an inevitability over which we have no control is an affront to human pride and prowess. We are confident of our ability to create and construct. We devise ingenious devices for accomplishing our purposes in the arts as well as in the practical and technical facets of our existence. We become convinced that there is nothing which we cannot do given sufficient time and resources. Indeed we all appear to share the motto of the Navy's Seabees, "The difficult we do immediately, the impossible takes a little longer." Then right in the middle of our self-assurance comes the problem of death.[1] Extraordinary efforts at control as in cryogenics where a body is deep-frozen awaiting a cure for the disease from which it died do not eliminate an uneasy awareness that we have run up against a mystery for which there is ultimately no solution, an event which is not finally subject to our mastery. The institutionalization of death industries such as funeral directing may be an attempt to hide the insistence of such a condition. This conclusion or insight may be derived from Robert Fulton and Gilbert Geis' comments

> By assigning professional functionaries the responsibility for traditional familial roles, contemporary society not only avoids direct and disconcerting contact with death itself, but also, more important, permits its members to avoid close and disturbing confrontations with the inconsistencies inherent in the traditional theological explanations and emerging secular viewpoints. In current secular societies death is not considered an open or polite topic of conversation except among the aged, and the dead are hidden from view as quickly as possible and removed to a funeral home at the first opportunity. (68–69)

I have found no more beautifully lyrical expression of the revulsion a person may feel with all the artificiality which may surround the process of preparing a body for an open casket funeral than Joseph Mathews telling of "The Time my Father Died" (4–9). Mathews speaks of his seething outrage at seeing the mortician's mockery before him and of his own wistful attempt to cleanse his father's face and restore the marks and wrinkles of his long and eventful life which the gaudy cosmetics had garishly sought to cover.

While most persons in our society shy away from any involvement with the dead body of a loved one, there are those who go against the prevailing social practices of turning the final ministrations over to the professionals. I am reminded of one of my early hospice patient's wife. She had not wanted a volunteer. She was a self-reliant person who, having lost one husband to death, believed she could handle this alone. She eventually consented and as I sat by her husband's bedside and he and I communicated with our eyes and squeezing one another's hands she grew to accept the role I could play. In fact, she called me at 7:00 am on a Saturday morning and told me that her husband had died about midnight. She went on to say that she took off his soiled pajamas and bed clothes, bathed and dressed him in fresh clothes and shaved him and sat beside him through the rest of the night. The undertakers came about 8:00 am that morning to remove his body. What a heroic and humane act of human love and devotion which few of us are able to accomplish today!

In the face of death religion can assist us in appreciating the grandeur of man's finite existence without succumbing to the grandiose idolatry of an illusory infiniteness. Being powerful in many things does not translate into our having power over all things including death. The temptation to believe in our independent mastery over all things is belied by the realization that death is the symbol that though we may do a lot we cannot do all things by our own efforts. We did not give ourselves physical or biological birth nor have we been able to live without the continual contributions of others throughout our lives. Facing death we are made aware of our common humanity which is both our glory and our humiliation, our grandeur and our misery as David Roberts has phrased it.[2]

The meaning of death which has had the longest association with religion is that of fear of punishment in an after-life. This meaning is not limited to Western civilization as we noted earlier. Buddhism, in for example the Japanese *Jigoku Soshi* (Hell Scroll) has vividly gruesome hells not far from the descriptions of Dante's *Inferno.*[3] Belief in an after-life has exerted an immense influence on human culture. It has served in long stretches of history to turn human attention from the here and now to the then and there. It has often left humankind unappreciative of the present and unconcerned with dealing with problems such as injustice, inequity, disease, or poverty. It has often made a sharp dichotomy between those who were reputed to have found the secret passageway or had the authority to dispense the tickets for the journey and those dependent upon their services. It was a method of social control whereby recalcitrants seeking to question the status quo could be brought into line by the threat of their souls roasting in hell for all eternity. Death was the sign of judgment which awaited all and made the threat a dreaded reality. Historic religions have found it easier to concentrate on the fear of punishment after death than on the joys of life well lived here and here-after.

Dealing with this meaning of death quickly becomes a theological matter. A person has to decide not only what he or she believes about life but also about the nature of God, creation, salvation, and all the other elements of religious faith. If God is seen as Absolute Sovereign on the model of a Medieval King then a person may cringe knowing that as a loyal subject he has no recourse but to accept the King's decrees even if these seal his damnation. Martin Luther's admonition to "let God be God" appears to be grounded in such a conviction of God's absolute sovereignty and leads to Luther's affirmation that he is willing to be "damned for the glory of God." How different is the conception of God as Agape, complete unconditional love, as Anders Nygren, Nels F.S. Ferre, John Templeton and others have labored to make clear. If God is conceived to be the Waiting Father whose nature is love, as in the parable of the prodigal son (Luke 15:11–32), then death may be seen as the surprising ecstasy of returning home. Helmut Thielicke opens this possibility up beautifully in his book *The Waiting Father*. Religion can help us look honestly at our beliefs about life as we face death and point us toward the resources of faith. In the Judaeo-Christian tradition these resources are primarily the biblical message and the theological heritage.

[1] In Lawrence Ferlinghetti, *A Coney Island of the Mind* (1958). Ferlinghetti parodies the world as a beautiful place in poem #11 and ends it with the line, "Yes but then right in the middle of it comes the smiling mortician." p. 89.

[2] See *The Grandeur and Misery of Man* (1955) particularly pages 143–151.

[3] A copy of the Japanese *Jigoku Soshi* (Hell Scroll) may be found in H.W. Janson, *History of Art* (1969), Color-plate 87 on page 576.

Chapter 3

Biblical Insights on the Mystery of Death

Jews, Christians, and Muslims are called "people of the Book". Their sacred scriptures play an indispensable role in their origin and development. Their scriptures are considered the primary source of knowledge and understanding of the divine human relationship, therefore perpetually relevant. Since each of these is a historical religion contending that God acts in history, their sacred scripture is considered the foundational account of God's creative and sustaining activity in history.

Theological exploration in each of these religions makes reference to and uses the biblical material as a touchstone. The Hebrew Scripture, which Christians refer to as the Old Testament, is essential for understanding the New Testament. The first scripture of the New Covenant Community was the Old Testament. Though there were leaders such as Marcion in the second century who tried to cut Christianity loose from the Old Testament, it has remained an inseparable part of the Christian scripture.

Old Testament treatments of the mystery of death[1]

Whether we start at Genesis or begin with an approach of historical criticism the Old Testament assumes God as the basic reality by which all else is understood. There is no argument for God's existence as in the philosophical approach of the Greeks. There is only the assertion of faith: "In the Beginning God created the heavens and the earth." God is the active force or power by which all else comes to be what it is. He is the Lord and Giver of Life, or as G. Ernest Wright put it, "The God who Acts." God, otherwise called Yahweh (YHWH) or in its tetra-grammaton the Lord (Adonai), is not a deity severed from the world or standing over against it. Nature is God's creation. God and Nature are not one reality as for the philosopher Baruch Spinoza. The Old Testament knows nothing of pantheism. The whole of creation is not equal to the sum of its parts. It is more like panentheism in which every aspect of nature may become a means of revealing the God who created it and stands behind it. God is not conceived as a nature god or as the summation of the natural order. He is not to be equated with any or all aspects of the natural world. God has created whatever is in nature.

When speaking of God we are limited by our historic and linguistic concepts. It would be good to remind ourselves at this point that as the Medieval theologians were bold to point out God is *sui generis*, that is, in a class by himself. Our language refers to things we know or experience and thus we use anthropomorphic terms knowing that these do not literally apply to God. These terms are the bridge between our experiences and our deepest convictions about the nature of God. For example, since we create we use the term creation to refer to God's activity. Since we are capable of loving, we speak of God not only as loving but as a Being whose very nature is Love. Since we act in a historical context of time and space we refer to God as a God who acts in history. It was a basic conviction of the biblical writers that God acts in the affairs of history so that even the events which happen at man's initiative are expressions of divine agency.

Human history is the arena of God's most characteristic nature. God creates human beings in his own image with the capacity to create, to control, to fulfill, to act responsibly, and to love. God calls men and women out of the security of their comfortable existence to venture into the unknown terrain of new and promising territory. God sustains us in our search for ourselves and through a continually renewed covenant establishes the basis of faithfulness by which we develop a sense of community for fulfillment. God comes to be known in the experiences of human beings in history whether in wilderness wanderings or amidst the tumultuous struggles for becoming a nation for whom He is the High and Holy One. God is not known apart from the experiences by which men and women come to know themselves. These experiences become revelatory for us in our quest for meaningful human life.

The Old Testament treats the existence of God as a reality to be accepted rather than as a proposition to be reasoned about. Human life is approached as dynamic and relational rather than as static or independent. God breathes into men and women the breath of life and they become living persons. Human life is one of closeness to the source of its vivification, of covenant with God the Giver of Life.[2]

Men and women like God from whom they receive their life are multidimensional-unities. They are whole human beings. Human problems are characteristically approached not as isolated events having greater or lesser significance in relating to God but as expressions of the fundamental covenantal relationship between God the Giver and human beings as the recipients of life. Men and women are seen from various perspectives such as body, soul, mind, or heart. None of these receives preferential treatment in understanding the relationship of humans to the divine. It is not that a human being *has* a body, a soul, a heart, a mind. A human being *is* a body, a soul, a heart, a mind. A whole human being is given life and from him or her life is taken away. Life is a sacred reality more basic than soul, body, or mind. These are but ways in which the unity of a man's or woman's being is known and expresses itself. No part, whether body, soul, heart, or mind, has an eternal or immortal nature. Its unity does not come from a pre-established ontology to which the actions of God and human beings conform, but from an ontology of creative action in which life is created expressing its divine origin and destiny. Life is relational and the idea of an immortal part unaffected by the transitoriness of human existence is foreign to the Old Testament.

Men and women live because they have been created by God in a vitalizing or covenantal relationship. The Old Testament for the most part avoids ideas of human beings known or understood as separated individuals. A man or woman is a person-in-relation to God the Giver of life. Since this is the situation of all men and women, they are thereby in relation to one another. The idea of corporate personality functions for human beings in society much the same as the idea of a man or woman as a multidimensional unity. It expresses the profound awareness that nothing including human life can be understood as an isolated entity. Isolation or brokenness is a distorted condition where one is separated from the source of his or her vitality. In this light sin is not an act of insult or moral petulance. It is life disoriented from its creative ground or origin resulting in strained relations with God, the community, and the unity of one's own being. Life in community is basic. The concept of the Kingdom of God where the divisiveness of life, its brokenness and distortions are overcome, arose not as a result of failure to achieve lasting political independence but as the logical extension of the conviction that men and women belong to one another because they belong first and forever to God.

Death in the Old Testament is seen relative to basic faith assertions. God is the Vivifier and men and women are the recipients of vitality. A religious, symbolic, or mythic interpretation rather than a scientific or biological one is offered in the Old Testament. The biblical material is concerned primarily with the *meaning* of human death rather than its facticity which it assumes.

Death is the removal of God's spirit (*ruach*). Sin and death were assumed to be aspects of the same religious phenomenon. Sin is the proximate or relative dimension of the separation of man or woman from God. Death is the final or absolute separation. Life is the fullness of relationship to God and long life on this earth was the sign of God's favor. Death is the withdrawal of God's vitalizing spirit. Natural death coming at the end of a long and prosperous life was not a terror from which one wished to flee. It was the expected and accepted outcome of the relationship. In death the whole person died as in life the whole person had been vitalized. Death was not the liberation of an immortal soul from a transitory or temporal body in which it had been enslaved or imprisoned. Body was but another of the dimensions by which the goodness of life was manifest.

With the removal of the spirit (*ruach*), the soul (*nephesh*) and body (*basar*) came to their end. The soul may linger for a while as a shade going to the dark unknown of the "not land". This process was no different than the dissolution of the body which could be observed taking place as a consequence of death. In time the "not land" took on qualities of a realm of deep darkness (*Sheol*) where the shades of former selves lived until their vitality was completely exhausted or extinguished.[3] For a long time this was the only concept of an afterlife in the Old Testament. Religious faith did not necessitate a belief in a meaningful after-life. The prime tenet of faith was the relationship with God not a metaphysical structure assuring an answer to death. As Lou Silberman points out:

> Whatever ideas about and attitudes toward death the Israelites held, such ideas and attitudes stood in some crucial relationship to what they believed about life; and that in turn was related to other spheres of interest until as D.R.G. Owen has suggested, these were ultimately connected to a way of understanding God. (14)

Death was a real event in which fact and meaning coalesced as the activity of God. The Psalmist could ask whether there was anywhere he could flee from God's presence:

> Where can I go from your spirit?
> Or where can I flee from your presence?
> If I ascend to heaven, you are there;
> If I make my bed in Sheol, you are there.
> If I take the wings of the morning and
> settle at the farthest limits of the sea,
> Even there your hand shall lead me,
> and your right hand shall hold me fast. (Psalm 139:
> 7–10 RSV)

Faith was posited on the presence of God and the answer to death was to be found in trusting in Him.

Trust for the Old Testament writers was what today is termed existential commitment. It was not resignation or surrender whereby a person acknowledging that he had no alternative turned reluctantly to accept the reign of God over his life. It was acceptance of the presence of God as the source of a person's integrity often after intense struggle and acute conflict, Such was the case of Job. Among the tragic sufferings of his struggle, death stands as the symbol for the problem of loss and assault against the meaningfulness of relationship to God. Since death comes also to the righteous, is that not justification for abandoning the religious life? Is not a person as well off admitting either that he or she has sinned and by that sin brought upon himself or herself the anguish of suffering and death? Should he or she not accept without question the easy formula that since God gives life He may also take it away at any time without any other explanation or rationale than divine action? Would not a person be wise to seize the day for eating, drinking and pursuing happiness through indulgent pleasures? If Job is to maintain his integrity, can he acknowledge sins he has not committed for the sake of comfort in his loss as his friends urge him to do? Hardly! Tenaciously he refuses to submit to their pleading, convinced that the answer to death is not to be found in lying about his own human experience. The Deuteronomic formula which had served so many so well for so long—the belief that the religious life is rewarded with prosperity, happiness, and longevity—was no longer acceptable to Job if it ever had been. What courage it must have required to have stood against the pressuring of his well-meaning orthodox friends who found it impossible to even raise the questions so necessary to Job. Job sought a reasonable answer to a central human mystery. This was not characteristic of the Old Testament. The quest for an explanation of meaningless suffering was equally a quest for an answer to the problem of meaningless death. Must a person sacrifice either his intelligence or his integrity in grappling with suffering and death? If the epilogue is omitted as an addendum by those who could not be content with Job's resolution, then the mystery is still baffling, the question still intense. However, it is no longer experienced without existential support in meeting it. What was accepted without being internalized is given up for an acceptance of a first-hand personal relationship with the God who can be trusted in the mysteries of life and death.

The solution comes not in an abstract rationalization of the problem but in a trust at the mysterious center of one's life.

Similarly the writer of the 73rd Psalm offers a religious rather than a philosophical answer. There is nothing in the nature of reality which reduces the threat of death by subsuming it in an eternal cycle. Death is still the real and final event it had been all along for the Old Testament writers. Its reality is accepted with the confidence that God is not far from us in the experiences of life of which death is the last act. In the face of injustices and death itself one can trust in God. No picture is drawn of human fate after death nor is a person offered the assurance that everything will turn out all right in the end. Having committed oneself to God in life one can trust Him in death. This trust maintains the meaningfulness of the event.

In cases like these religion is the life lived to cope with death. It is a life of obedience to instruction, faithfulness to God's guidance, an ordered yet free and responsible life signified by Torah in the Old Testament. How unfortunate that Christians and sometimes Jewish scholars have parodied such a life by reducing Torah either to restrictive law or limiting it to the first five books of the Hebrew Scripture (*TANAKH*). The first five books are Torah for in them the relationship of trust between men and women and God is archetypal in the encounters of Abraham, Isaac, Jacob, Joseph, and Moses. It is *the life of trust* about which these books write not the record itself which is preeminent. The same is true of Torah as law. Law is the ordered context of the life of trust in which the terms of interdependence and responsibility are set forth enabling a person to live a life of trust. It is not the law *per se* which is sacred but life which law is designed to protect and enhance. The same could be said of covenant which for many biblical scholars is the hermeneutical paradigm. Covenant is contrasted with contract: in a contract the obligations and advantages of both parties are spelled out as completely as possible demanding full adherence if the benefits and burdens are to ensue. A covenant, on the other hand, is a relationship of commitment of two parties to one another in which the specifics cannot all be anticipated nor defined. At its simplest it was stated: "I will be your God and you will be my people." That is to say, "wherever we are going, we are going there together." Covenant is for the sake of a meaningful life in which giving and receiving necessary for responsible freedom and human integrity are assured. The Old Testament points up religion's order of priorities for humanizing life. A man or woman is religious, that is, trusts God for the sake of fulfilling his or her humanity, not the reverse. Human life need not be sacrificed either literally or symbolically to the acculturated and institutionalized forms of religion. The forms are important as means to realization of life in Torah. As the prophet Ezekiel noted, even the dried bones and lost hopes of lifeless religion could be transformed by the life-giving spirit to bring human beings out of their dead faithlessness.

New Testament treatments of the mystery of death[4]

New Testament treatments are basically continuous with the Old Testament though points of difference and discontinuity can be maintained. The primary difference is Jesus as the Christ embodying the teachings and message of the Jewish heritage.

Jesus of Nazareth drew richly from his own religious heritage contending against those whose iconoclastic zeal wanted to abolish the past. He assured his hearers that he had come not to destroy the Law and the Prophets but to fulfill them. (Matthew 5:17) From the Prophet Isaiah he read the text of his programmatic sermon—to bring good news to the poor, proclaim release to the captives and recovery of sight to the blind, to let the oppressed go free and to proclaim the year of the Lord's favor. (Luke 4:18–19). He gathered about him a group of disciples whose religious background was for the most part homogeneous with his own. He was appalled at the way his contemporaries had lost the vitality of their faith and fallen prey to making religion a mere formality. The living relationship with God and its effect on daily life had been obscured by the acculturated residue of the faith of their fathers. From their common faith primary categories were drawn. When questioned about the heart of religion as eternal life he turned not to some new and esoteric teaching but to a recital of the Shema (Deuteronomy 6:4) accentuating the totality of the love of God and man derived from it. (Luke 10:25–28) It was essential that the teaching become enacted in life. This was a message which had been proclaimed in Israel for centuries.

To point men and women to the goal of human life he turned to his own religious reservoir proclaiming the Kingdom of God. There had been many erroneous interpretations of the expectations of such a realm. Many had made the concept into an expectation of a geo-political victory over their opponents. For them as for many others since then it was a way of righting the wrongs of the here and now on the plain of human history. However, Jesus drew upon another emphasis. He saw the Kingdom of God as a covenantal relationship in which men and women participate in the goodness of life because they are intimately bound together in the goodness of God.

Paul who set the direction of Christianity in its formative period had been a devoutly conscientious Jew. When he became a Christian he became an equally zealous opponent of Judaism. This change did not keep him from using the synagogue as a starting point for preaching the Christian message in his travels. At first it appeared that the new movement was but another sect in Judaism not unlike the Pharisees, Sadducees, Essenes or others. It became quickly apparent that there were irreconcilable differences particularly around the question of universalism versus particularism. The missionary fervor of the new faith was an embarrassment to Judaism which with the one exception of a brief period expressed in the Book of Jonah had never been a missionary religion. With the impetuosity of youth, it drew the lines sharply and cast its net widely to include all who were willing to respond favorably to the kerygma, or message of God's Kingdom. At the point of the kerygma Christianity and Judaism parted company opening a chasm which has still not been bridged and which is often overcome only by tentative and uncomfortable tolerance. Christians were saying that Jesus was the long awaited Messiah who had been crucified under the dual charges of blasphemy and insurrection but whom God had raised from the dead. From the start, Christians attributed to the crucifixion/resurrection event the significance of God's dual victory over man's twin enemies sin and death.

God was the God of the living so that even the event of death was powerless against Him. Religion was not capitulation to death in inconsolable remorse. It was a way of life for dealing with the human dilemmas of sin and death. The earliest Christian rituals were rituals of affirmation of the Living God having conquered death by raising Christ from the dead. Baptism was a dramatic and symbolic reenactment of the event of death as the believer was buried with Christ in the baptismal water. Death could not have the last word. As they were buried with Christ so they were raised with him to a new life. The community shared in that affirmation each time it celebrated the eucharist proclaiming the essential relationship of men and women with God in Christ. God was not some remote First Cause or abstract philosophical principle actualizing itself out of eternity in time. God was for the early Christian community the God and Father of our Lord Jesus Christ. No other name than this is given for God in the New Testament. Attempts at defining God's nature culminated in the concise affirmation that God is love and love is the way of life to which men and women are called. (I John 4:8)

Jesus was calling men and women to life in the Kingdom of God. It was a life of love for themselves and their neighbors. Its source was in their relationship with the God of the living who is Himself love, not in their innate goodness. Jesus was the life-bringer as he declared to them: "I am come that they might have life and that they might have it more abundantly." (John 10:10) Religion was supportive of life, not the other way around, as Jesus obliquely said: "the Sabbath was made for man, not man for the Sabbath." (Mark 2:27) The same applied to the whole range of religious phenomena. Jesus' objective was not to produce a new religion to which they should be unwaveringly obedient. It was instead to assist them in discovering the rich resources of religious faith for living. These resources would free them for the fullness of human life enabling them to overcome the threats, fears, and incapacities which sin and death set in their way. Jesus enjoyed life and caused the pious great consternation by his apparent irreligion and casualness regarding certain moral restrictions. He talked freely about life and death and boldly proclaimed that he was "the resurrection and the life" (John 11:25a). He maintained that the life he lived came from God and was so qualitatively significant that death was ultimately powerless to extinguish it.

Jesus acknowledged the reality of death. He comforted his grieving friend Martha by saying, "those who believe in me, even though they die, will live." (John 11:25b) When these words appeared much like the comfort the promise the Sadducees held out for a resurrection in the last day he emphasized the present reality of life beyond death in its qualitative dimensions. Leander Keck approaches it from a different angle when he maintains that Jesus shifted the ground of talk about death refusing to "speculate about the death of those whose life was snuffed out, just as he refused to speculate about the nature of the post-resurrection existence." (43)

Henry Cadbury saw Jesus' comments on life after death as "incidental":

> It was not a major concern of Jesus to expound or reassert the views of the future life which he held or shared. His references to it are mainly incidental, and associated in a subordinate way with his major interests....Even the Kingdom of God for all its frequency of mention in our records is not the central concern of the Gospels. The same may be said of the resurrection or 'eternal life'. (134)

Jesus had already experienced the life which refuses to let death be the last word and talking about it was not preeminent.

This experience did not remove the terror of death either for Jesus or for those who followed him. The dark night of the soul could only be lived through with the cry, "My God, my God why have you forsaken me? (Mark 15:34) In the agony of death Jesus calls out with the words of the Psalmist (Psalm 22:1) which begins in despair but ends in victory: "Posterity will serve him; future generations will be told about the Lord, and proclaim his deliverance to a people yet unborn, saying that he has done it" (Psalm 22: 30–31). The cry of despair was a prelude to hope. It was only fitting that Jesus would find his religious heritage his most natural resource in the event of his death. The cry of death was the prelude to life not as easy continuity but as the revivifying miracle of resurrection, which was as mysterious to comprehend as birth itself grounded not on reasoned ontological necessity of human immortality but on God's faithful gift of life eternal.

This gift of life meets its greatest obstacle for faith in the stubborn fact of death. Leander Keck, having taken the position that death was not a central concern for Jesus, obviously does not see death as a major obstacle:

> Jesus did not regard death as an obstacle to faith in God or as the crucial dimension about man that must be overcome. Death is a qualifier of man's existence, and as such makes life so precious that there is no equivalent for it: What will a man give in exchange for his life? The answer is clear not because Jesus believed in the 'life-principle' or because he believed in the immortality of the soul but because he saw that life was bounded by inevitable death. The insecurity of life, which the ever-present possibility of death represents, should lead to repentance, to a Godward turning of one's life. (42)

Death comes to all men and women religious and irreligious alike. Death is the last enemy not alone for human beings but for God as well. Since God is the Giver of life, death which takes away life is an assault on the power of God. God has called men and women into being and has breathed into them the breath of life. In Jesus the Christ he has come that they might have life which death cannot destroy. What then is to become of God when it is so obvious that each person dies? Death is the absolute separation akin to but also different from all the other relative separations of life. Religion must provide means of dealing with the mystery of sin and death the proximate and ultimate enemies of the relationship of men and women to God.

The New Testament finds its answer to this problem as did the Old Testament in a life of faith in God. To come to a realization that true life is in being related to God is to come also to the realization that whether a person lives or whether he dies he is God's. He is the Lord's and nothing can separate him from "the love of God in Christ Jesus our Lord". (Romans 8:39) Nothing in life or death is greater than the God who has provided for both of these. Death is the last enemy, but death is not outside the context of the power of God. Triumphantly the early church proclaimed that neither death nor life would be able to separate a man or woman from the love of God eternally alive in Christ Jesus.

For the Christian it is this life of faith symbolized in commitment to God through Jesus as the Christ that is the answer to death. In the Old Testament such a life of faith was symbolized in the life of Torah. Torah with its attendant stress on obedience, responsible freedom, covenant, and life in community was for the Old Testament the appropriate religious response. For the New Testament such a life was symbolized as life in Christ who becomes the way to life eternal. This way is entered into though not fully experienced in time and space in the here and now. It is a life of faith, hope, and love in which love becomes the way for filling out the content of the life of faith and the grounding of hope that such a life once having been entered into will find its fulfillment beyond the narrow passage of death.

Arnold Toynbee has a fascinating treatment of this experience of life coming to human beings through the immortality of the divine being in whom a believer gains life beyond death. To be a god is to be immortal, that is, not to be subject to death. Toynbee asserts:

> To be exempt from death is, in man's eyes, the prime qualification for being regarded by man as being super human....the belief that a god is not subject to death threatens to open up an unbridgeable spiritual gulf between the god and his human worshipper. If the god has not shared, and is *ex officio* exempt from sharing with man an experience that is a human being's most formidable ordeal, how can the god enter into man's feelings in the face of death, and how can he then be a 'very present help' to man in coping with the most grievous of all man's troubles? The god in whom man longs to believe, with whom he is eager to get into personal touch, and for whom he is moved to feel an extreme devotion is a god who is immortal, yet who, paradoxically, has nevertheless shared with his worshippers the human experience of death....Man's adoration of a

god who has died and has then asserted his immortality by coming to life again rises to its acme when the god is believed to have suffered death voluntarily and deliberately. (*Man's Concern with Death*, 67–68)

Toynbee then particularizes his general observations about a universal religious phenomenon of divine immortality in the historic religious manifestation of Christianity. This conclusion would be appropriate except that Christianity did not maintain that Jesus was immortal and could not die—in fact it considered this a heresy. It maintained instead that through Christ's death and resurrection human beings gained life eternal beginning here and now and reaching beyond death. Though there is disagreement on Jesus being immortal, Toynbee expresses something valuable when he says, "The Christian's feeling for Christ gives the full measure of man's concern with the problem and ordeal with which the fact of death confronts a human being." (*Man's Concern with Death*, 68)

It is appropriate at this point to remember Athanasius' brilliant affirmation that "unless he had become like us; we could not have become like him". That is, unless Jesus Christ had come as a human being subject to human death, human beings could not enter into the divine transformation of death into life eternal which only God could bring about.[5]

Immortality or resurrection?[6]

In both philosophy and the popular mind immortality is the favored way of responding to human mortality. When the biblical perspective is taken seriously, it becomes important to take a look at the distinction between immortality and resurrection. Oscar Cullman's work has been pivotal for that distinction which differentiates between death related to immortality and death answered by resurrection. Cullman contrasts the Greek concept as epitomized in the death of Socrates with the biblical or Judaeo-Christian expression epitomized in the death of Jesus. For the Greeks, men and women are eternal souls inhabiting a temporal body loaned to it for a brief journey in time and space. Plato sees the body as the prison-house of the soul. Since the soul is eternal or permanent, it is not subject to the ravages of time, impermanence, or change. The crucial philosophical problem of permanence and change found its reconciliation in Plato's development of the two worlds of eternity and time. In the eternal world from which the soul has descended pure ideas or forms exist. In the temporal world into which the soul has descended all is a matter of change or flux, as Heraclitus maintained. Change cannot perpetuate itself endlessly thus there must be a carrier something which while displaying the evidences of subjugation to change is in reality actually unchangingly continuous. Continuity was assured not by making the process of change absolute but by positing a reality so firmly grounded in the absolute that appearances were at least one step removed from reality. Discontinuity or change could exist only because there was continuity which both preceded and succeeded it. The body belonging to the world of space and time was passing away but the soul was traveling toward the realm of pure form or idea from which it had come. Socrates' with firm serenity and quiet confidence makes his statement after the Assembly has found him guilty and sentenced him to death. He says, "I go to death and you to life, which is better I do not know". There is an underlying belief in the soul's imperviousness to the debilitations of death. The body would pass away, dissolve, and decay. He could respond to his grieving disciples that they could do with his body as they saw fit since he would no longer be there after his death. The soul, on the other hand, would not be affected by such temporal conditions and would be set free to return to the eternal realm from which it had come at birth.[7]

In contrast the biblical experience posited upon a holistic anthropology held to the multidimensional unity of man. Death could not be the release of the soul by means of the dissolution of the body since body and soul were not separable parts. Death was the last enemy of man bringing all that he had been to its finality. No part of a human being was independently continuous since there were no parts. Man was a whole being ideally unified but in actual human existence often lacking integration. Death was the dissolution of the whole person who had come into being vivified by God in the miraculous act of birth.

The biblical writers went no further back in their ontology than "in the beginning God." At the other end of the spectrum their response would be "in the end God." As Paul Irion observes:

> It is the Christian position that life, death, and life after death must be hopefully grounded in God's action. All three elements of existence are related to God's will and God's power. Christianity has rejected with consistency an understanding of man's immortality as confidence in an indomitable part of his nature and has preferred to think of life after death as resurrection; new life bestowed by God's mercy. (41)

A religion of life created by God "in the beginning" and re-created by God "in the end" not a metaphysic of soul, was the biblical writers' presupposition. The Greek philosophical approach was an ontological argument for the eternal existence of the soul. The biblical approach was an existential affirmation of life defined in relationship to God. It is the assumption on which all else rests.

In a way both the argument for immortality and the argument for resurrection seem specious to contemporary men and women who are convinced neither by the rationalism of the Greeks nor the affirmative existentialism of the Jews and Christians. Our scientific, technological world is grounded neither in the absolutes of eternity which find their approximations in time and space nor in the creationism of the biblical experience wherein God calls into being whatever is. As Krister Stendahl observes, a new mythological framework must be found:

> ...both immortality and resurrection in their original settings are ideas which require creative interpretation and demythologizing if they are to fit into any pattern of twentieth-century thought....Once both concepts are recognized as mythological, there is a new possibility of assessing the role and significance and truth of such linguistic symbols. (5–6)

The longing for a meaningful life in meeting death is not diminished by the inability of persons to accept either the wisdom of the Greeks or the commitment of the Judaeo-Christian approach. As Augustine noted, "we are conscious in ourselves of having a desire for eternal life."[8] Harry Wolfson responds to this:

> With such a desire, I imagine we are all still possessed and we should, therefore, quite naturally like to know what meaning for us today have these views of the Fathers on immortality and resurrection—especially for those of us today who think that we need a new kind of promise and a new kind of hope for a new kind of fulfillment of this our innate desire and longing for eternal life. (94)

Contemporary culture is caught between the loneliness of dreadful freedom carrying the full burden of responsibility for all humankind and wistful nostalgia of return to the simplicities and certainties of an age before future shock and incessant change. Lacking appreciation for the essential element of transcendence and God's presence many experience the absence of God and feel they have to go it alone. Though we may not be able to accept the mythological inheritance of immortality or resurrection we may learn from them the integrity of spirit which refuses to rest on the surface of existence and probes the questions of permanence and change. In this awesome situation of the basic relationship of life and death in a world with or without God we, like Jacob must wrestle with our angel (Genesis 32:24) until we find blessing in the struggle.

It is painful to remind ourselves that the present state of the arts, musical and literary as well as visual, reflects this transitional and anarchic experience. Much of Western artistic creation has been dependent on biblical and Greek mythologies centering on the mystery of death and the human response of either immortality or resurrection.[9] Oscar Cullman making his case for a reconsideration of the primacy of resurrection for the Christian faith noted:

> In this study I have referred more than once to the Isenheim altarpiece by the medieval painter Grunewald. It was the resurrection body that he depicted, not the immortal soul. Similarly, another artist, Johann Sebastian Bach, has made it possible for us to hear, in the Credo of the *Mass in B Minor*, the musical interpreta-

tion of the words of this ancient creed which faithfully
reproduces the New Testament faith in Christ's resurrection and our own. The jubilant music of this great
composer is intended to express not the immortality of
the soul but the event of the resurrection of the body....
And Handel, in the last part of the Messiah gives us
some inkling of what Paul understood by the sleep of
those who rest in Christ; and also, in the song of tri-
umph, Paul's expectation of the final resurrection when
the last trumpet shall sound and we shall be changed.
Whether we share this hope or not, let us at least admit
that in this case the artists have proved the best exposi-
tors of the Bible. (53)

We are heirs of a world which knows less and less of meaning stretching behind us with restorative appreciation for the
past or forward into creative anticipation of the future. We have
difficulty being faithful either to a vision of an eternal soul by
which truth, beauty, and goodness are manifesting themselves
or to a relationship to God which gives to us the meaning of our
being. Jacques Choron calls attention to an unexpected source
pinpointing the dilemma we observe:

Bertrand Russell has seen clearly the inadequacy of
purposes that do not transcend the scope of one's individual life or even of mankind: The world has need
of a philosophy, or a religion, which will promote life.
But in order to promote life it is necessary to value
something other than life. Life devoted only to life is
animal without any real human value, incapable of preserving men permanently from weariness and the feeling that all is vanity. If life is to be fully human it must
serve some end which seems, in some sense, outside
human life, some end which is impersonal and above
mankind, such as God or truth or beauty. Those who
best promote life do not have life for their purpose.
They aim rather at what seems like gradual incarnation, a bringing into our human existence of something
eternal, something that appears to imagination to life in
a heaven remote from strife and failure and the *devour-*

ing jaws of Time. Contact with this eternal world—even if it be only a world of our imagining—brings a strength and a fundamental peace which cannot be wholly destroyed by the struggles and apparent failures of our temporal life. (268)[10]

[1] The material in this section is based primarily on: Lou H. Silberman, "The Treatment of Death in the Old Testament," *Perspectives on Death,* (1970) Liston Mill, ed.; Ninian Smart, "Death in the Judaeo-Christian Tradition," *Man's Concern With Death* (1969), Arnold Toynbee et al, eds.; Robert Martin-Achard. *From Death to Life: a Study of the Development of the Doctrine of the Resurrection in the Old Testament* (1960), and Ludwig Kohler, *Hebrew Man* (1956).

[2] See Aubrey S. Johnson. *The Vitality of the Individual in the Thought of Ancient Israel* (1949).

[3] See Lou H. Silberman, "The Treatment of Death in the Old Testament," *Perspectives on Death* (1970). page 26.

[4] The material in this section is based primarily on: Leander Keck, "The Treatment of Death in the New Testament," *Perspectives on Death,* (1970), Liston Mill, ed.;. Ian Henderson, *Myth in the New Testament,* (1952). Hans Bartsch, *Kerygma and Myth* (1957). Henry S. Cadbury, "Intimations of Immortality in the Thought of Jesus," *Immortality and Resurrection* (1965). Krister Stendahl, ed.

[5] See Athanasius. *On the Incarnation* (1953).

[6] The material in this section is based primarily on: Oscar Cullman, "Immortality of the Soul or Resurrection of the Dead: the witness of the New Testament," *Immortality and Resurrection,* (1965) Krister Stendahl, ed.; James J. Heller, "The Resurrection of Man," *Theology Today* (July 1958); Roger Troisfontaines, "Death, a test for love, a condition of freedom," *Cross Currents.* (Summer 1957); and Hugh Vernon White, "Immortality and Resurrection in Recent Theology," *Encounter* (Winter 1961).

[7] For one of the most beautiful and heroic treatments of death and dying see Plato's recounting of Socrates' trial and death in the *Apology, Phaedo, and Crito.*

[8] Augustine is quoted in Harry Wolfson, "Immortality and Resurrection in the Philosophy of the Church Fathers," *Immortality and Resurrection* (1965) Krister Stendahl, ed. page 94.

[9] Additional insights are found in Frederick J. Hoffman, "Mortality and Modern Literature," *The Meaning of Death* (1959), Herman Feifel, ed.; Carla Gottlieb, "Modern Art and Death," *The Meaning of Death* (1959), Herman Feifel, ed.; and Amos N. Wilder, "Mortality

and Contemporary Literature," *The Modern Vision of Death* (1967). Nathan Scott, ed.

[10]Jacques Choron's quote from Bertrand Russell comes from Russell's *Principles of Social Reconstruction* (1916) published in the United States under the title *Why Men Fight* (1917).

Chapter 4

Theological Resources
for the Mystery of Death

Theology is the ongoing attempt of the intellectual life of the church to reinterpret the nature and significance of the relationship of the human and the divine. It must be done again in each new cultural context and era. In an economically oriented culture the divine human relationship is interpreted in economic metaphors of redemption, purchase, sale, contract, and transaction. In a feudal culture that relationship is interpreted in metaphors of satisfaction, fealty, allegiance and honor. In revolutionary times the metaphors are of radical upheaval, transformation, primal change, and freedom. Historical theology requires understanding the culture in which a theologian lives and works.

Often the major figures are theologians who out of passion for the significance of the gospel in response to a specific occasion or cultural event feel compelled to deal explicitly with a problem, topic, or issue. Later readers are often unaware of the original provocative event and seek to use the material without awareness of the circumstances of its origin. They want to make timeless truth out of time-full truths forgetting that the truths are most meaningful in the context of the response. It is important to try and enter vicariously into the lives and times of theologians if their thought is to be helpful in dealing with prominent issues. It is important to remember that when we look at theological treatments of death the expression and for-

mulations change, but the mystery of death remains as crucial
for us as it was for them.

The central formative event for Christianity was the cru-
cifixion/resurrection. The problem of death was at the core
rather than the periphery for early Christianity. Jesus Christ
had been put to death. He had died a young vigorous man who
had posed a threat to the established order in which he existed.
Religion and government both experienced the revolutionary
threat of his approach to life. Neither of them saw any way to
reconcile his appeal to the authentication of life by direct relationship to God in freedom and responsibility with their own
culturally validated and authorized institutions. Those institutions concluded "it is better for you that one man die for the
people than to have the whole nation destroyed" (John 11:50).
They saw him tearing apart the fabric of society by weaken-
ing those institutions through his direct and personal appeal to
God. His death was for them a solution to the culture's struggle
for continued life. However, his death did not eliminate the
basic conflicts between those whose divine-human relationship
was self-authenticating and those who found the religious and
political structures and orders of existence essential for their
meaningful life. For the followers of Jesus of Nazareth, his death
was a sign of defeat of the divine in its incursions into the human arena. Their return to their former homes to resume their
previous way of existence was the hopeless acceptance of the
inevitability of death as the last enemy of man. Man's ill-defined
but irrepressible yearning for the divine in the midst of and
beyond the human had been dealt a crushing blow with his
crucifixion. With the unanticipated surprise of the resurrection
they came to the conviction that death had not defeated life but
that God had taken death and made it the means of affirming
His lordship over all of life. Death no longer stood outside the
sphere of God's influence.

The God of the Living had raised Christ from the dead. In
doing so God had opened a way whereby men and women
could pass from death to life. Henry Cadbury points to the difference between Christ's resurrection and the resurrection of
his followers:

For others than Jesus resurrection was in the future, hence uncertain. With Jesus it was in the past, and 'only the past is secure.' But, along with the Holy Spirit it was a guarantee of the future. Both of them are called 'first fruits'. The resurrection of Jesus sets the pattern for other cases....What God had done, God could do. (120–121)

A new mythology arose for the small band of disciples. Its roots were in Judaism and the mystery religions which abounded in their culture. But it was new and powerful enough to become a world transforming reality. Unresolved questions were not capable of denying the myth by which they fashioned their lives.

It is advisable to interrupt here for a moment to clarify the use of the word myth or mythic. In our culture it usually connotes something which is false, contrived, illusory, or made-up. In the religious sense the term myth is a way of seeing which organizes basic convictions, intuitions, and impressions about life around memorable stories. Every age has its mythos. Some ages, such as ours, are iconoclastic transitional periods which persist in ridiculing or destroying the myths of the past without being able to formulate new myths capable of giving unity and power to a society.

With resounding boldness the earliest Christians saw the myth of Christ's crucifixion/resurrection as the most unshakable pivotal point of their new life. He who had died was now alive and they too would pass from death to life because of him. As Cadbury perceptively expressed it, "The effect of the belief in Jesus' resurrection on the early Christian belief in the wider resurrection experience can hardly be overestimated." (122) Because Jesus had been raised by God's re-creative act, his followers looked forward to a time when they too would be raised.

This was the heart-felt pulsation that drove them into the Roman world with missionary zeal and fervor. This mythic event of death's defeat, along with the role of sin and guilt leading to judgment on the other side of death, would be the basis of all else that followed for Christianity through the centuries.

After the Time of the New Testament

As Christianity spread from its birthplace in Palestine's Hellenized-Roman-Hebraic culture, it had to deal with the foundational myth in the light of the philosophical worldview and political realities of the lands into which it moved. It was not surprising that in such a syncretistic age the central problem of death found no single solution in theological interpretation.

Imperial Rome had developed law to a major science while appropriating from the Greeks and other conquered peoples achievements by which the ancient Mediterranean world had lived. A legalistic perspective would play a major role in the development of Christian theology. However, the whole question of the relationship of biblical revelation and Greek philosophy would be the more urgent issue confronting Christianity. The biblical myth of the crucifixion/resurrection was at the heart of the Christian faith and since it necessitated a commitment to the sovereign power and mercy of God it would run headlong into the insistence of the Romans that the Emperor was the sovereign power. Could belief in the resurrection be reconceived in terms of the more acceptable philosophical belief in immortality of the soul of the Greco-Roman world? Harry Wolfson noted that almost immediately that question was before them.

> But whatever one may be pleased to prove with regard to what Jesus thought of immortality and resurrection, to the Fathers of the Church these two beliefs were inseparably connected with each other. To them, the belief that Jesus rose on the third day after the Crucifixion meant that his soul survived the death of the body and was reinvested with his risen body….And this conception of resurrection as implying immortality was attributed by the Fathers also to Jesus. (55–56)

Wolfson continues, making a distinction between philosophical and scriptural immortality,

> To Plato, immortality belonged to the soul by nature, for by its very nature the soul could not be mortal. In Scripture, immortality was a gift or grace of God to the soul, for by its own nature the soul was mortal.

This distinction between the Platonic and the scriptural conception of immortality is constantly stressed by the Fathers. (57)

Could this distinction be useful for the Church's nascent theology? Could Roman legal categories be utilized to give substance to the divine-human relationship with which Christianity was concerned? Could Athens and Jerusalem find a way of living with one another without one being subsumed by the other?

For many early leaders of the Church such questions were distantly academic. Polycarp, for example, headed toward Rome for martyrdom in the arena where he would face lions to be "ground into flour for the Lord's loaf". It is sufficient to believe that, for him, the death of his Lord was assurance that he too would find a greater reality beyond death. Death was the cherished opportunity to bear witness to his faith and the faithfulness of God sustaining him against the worst that men could inflict upon him. Early on the Church concluded not only that "the blood of the martyrs is the seed of the church" but that the martyr's death brought immediate reward from God with the crown of life in paradise.[1] We must not, however, succumb to the temptation to view all the ancient history of Christianity as a martyrs' festival. Life had other less heroic and more prosaic problems.

The issue of a rapprochement between Athens and Jerusalem asserted itself frequently. Alexandria was the center of those confrontations where one side believed God had intended that He be worshipped as surely with a dedicated mind as with an impassioned heart and the other side contended that God's relation to human beings as recounted in the scripture was exclusive.[2]

Theologians like Origen found the philosophy of Plato compatible with the biblical record. Origen went to great lengths developing an elaborate mythology of death including a pretemporal fall and a resplendent angelic paradise leading to universal salvation. The Church rejected this view as heretical. But Origen was a glorious heretic who took seriously the problem of death and humanity's need to confront human death in the larger context of God's cosmic dimensions. Werner Jaeger overstates the case, but is worth listening to, when he says:

> The most important fact in the history of Christian doctrine was that the father of Christian theology, Origen, was a Platonic philosopher at the School of Alexandria. He built into Christian doctrine the whole cosmic drama of the soul, which he took from Plato, and although later Christian Fathers decided that he took over too much, that which they kept was still the essence of Plato's philosophy of the soul. (112)

At the other end of the theological spectrum stood Tertullian who had been a lawyer before he became a theologian. He was never able to see theology except from a legalistic perspective. For him, God had set down His requirements clearly and plainly. When a man met those requirements, he or she "put God in his debt." Out of this approach developed the treasury of merit crucial to the medieval world view in which the excess good deeds of the saints could be stored up and attributed to others to mitigate their deficiency in living up to God's standards. The direction of western Christian theology from Tertullian onward took a decided turn for legalism with stress on sin, guilt, and condemnation. Tertullian saw death as the determining event in the divine human relationship. Everything must be right with God at the time of that event. It was not the totality of one's life but the state in which one stood at the moment of death that determined whether a person went to heaven or hell. The function of the church was therefore to call men and women to accountability by offering them baptism as the seal of passage from life through death to the after-life. Baptism would not only absolve them from their sins and relieve them of their guilt, it would guarantee them acceptance by God who could not judge against them since they had done what he commanded even if it were done at the final moment of life. This legalistic focus on sin and guilt prevailed in Western Christianity not only in Roman Catholicism but in much of Protestantism centuries later. Death was then a secondary or derivative problem. In contrast to this belief, Eastern Christianity became more metaphysical, theatrical, liturgical, and dramatic than dogmatic. Death rather than sin and guilt was Eastern Orthodox Christianity's primary focus.

Augustine, Bishop of Hippo

It would be fascinating to look at the contributions of many other theologians, but we will concentrate on only a few as we proceed with this development. No one looms any larger on the theological horizon after the Apostle Paul than Augustine, Bishop of Hippo. His influence pervades the ancient, medieval, and modern worlds. Not only Thomas Aquinas in the thirteenth century but Martin Luther and John Calvin in the sixteenth century and Neo-Reformation/Neo-Orthodox theologians such as Reinhold Niebuhr in the twentieth century found him indispensable. His influence spread beyond theology affecting literary and psychological circles as well.

Much of Augustine's thought was expressed to deal with specific issues of an occasion. The Donatist and Pelagian controversies were occasions for significant development in his thought. In his *Confessions* he vividly describes his own spiritual development though Platonism, Manichaeism, and Neo-Platonism. His other major work, *The City of God,* was probably the more crucial for the problem of death. He lived in the time when the Roman Empire was falling apart. In such a time of societal disintegration many cried out for a reasonable explanation of the collapse. Augustine sought to answer the charge that the acceptance of Christianity and abandonment of Roman religion had brought about the fall in the early 5th century. In this context it was not the death of the individual with which Augustine was primarily concerned but the death of a culture. The Pauline conviction that "the wages of sin is death" is taken out of an individualistic framework and set in a theological perspective of world history. Cultures are infused with the seeds of their own death because all human good has a way of being perverted, distorted, and defiled. Whatever human beings create is infected with excessive pride or "concupiscence" as he calls it. The cities or cultures which they create are built on the force of power and power is insatiable. Nations become imperialistic as their greed and lust leads to concentration of wealth and influence in ever fewer leaders who lose their sense of equity and justice in governing others. Cultures, as well as the governments which maintain them, are weakened in their internal relations and fall prey to these same corrupted designs. Such is the situation of 'the city of man".

On the other hand, the city of God is characterized by conditions leading not to death but to life in brotherhood where love for one another and charity (caritas) is the hallmark. Each person is concerned more with the welfare of others than with his or her own well-being. Love, joy, and peace prevail rather than hate, despair and strife. Trust replaces suspicion and turmoil. It is not easy to discern the boundaries of the two cities. Augustine was ambiguous about the bounds of the city of God making it possible for the Medieval Church to identify itself with that city. Holding the keys to the kingdom of God it stood above and against all temporal powers which expressed the powers of death. The Church became the realm where men and women found life leading to an answer to death beyond the inevitable destruction and decay of the secular city of man.

In other works such as sermons, commentaries, and the *Confessions* Augustine devoted his attention to the deaths of men and women as individuals. Particularly helpful is his treatise *On the Immortality of the Soul.*[3] Like most of the early Fathers of the Church, Augustine dealt with death by attempting to follow both the biblical centrality of the resurrection and the philosophical position of the immortality of the soul. Harry Wolfson makes this clear:

> What Augustine's own conception of immortality was may be gathered from his statement that though 'the soul of man is, according to a peculiar sense of its own (*secundum quemdam modus suum*) immortal,' it is not absolutely immortal as God is, of whom it is written that he 'alone hath immortality' and as he proceeds he explains that the soul is described as being, 'according to a peculiar sense of its own, immortal' and as 'not wholly ceasing to live by its own nature' only that it is not annihilated, that is to say, it is not annihilated by God, who by his will had brought it into existence and who could, therefore, annihilate it, if he so willed. (60)

These views on human death were never adequately reconciled in Augustine's thought nor unique to him. His greater contribution lay in the paradigm of the death of culture which has had more direct bearing on western history.

Thomas Aquinas

Augustine represents the classical theological struggle in the ancient world. Thomas Aquinas is the prototype of the theological struggles of the medieval world and the theological embodiment of the gothic image. Gothic architecture elaborately depicted a world hierarchically reaching from its solid base on earth to its ever lighter and higher aspiration toward heaven. To the solid natural world was added the more ethereal supernatural world. Similarly in literature in Dante's *The Divine Comedy*, the heavier earthbound relationships give way to spiritualized stretches of the divine-human relationship. Culturally the medieval world was one which had found a new way of creation in stone and glass of cathedrals, picturesque literary imagery, and the architectonic theology of Aquinas.

The excitement of incorporating the philosophical base of Aristotle into Christian thought intrigued Aquinas. Like Augustine before him, Aquinas felt it necessary to give attention to biblical material. The resurrection because it was recorded in scripture was vigorously affirmed and defended. By the thirteenth century a number of events had shifted stress away from the resurrection to concentration on the immortality of the soul. The doctrine of purgatory had emerged as the sacramental system of the church expanded. The supremacy of the papacy and the powers of priests, bishops, and archbishops in dealing with death had grown stronger.

Augustine had taken two cities as his focal point; Aquinas took as his prime concern two orders of existence—the order of nature corresponding to Aristotle's material or physical world and the metaphysical order of super-nature or grace.

The soul is that entity which "actualizes the body as its matter." Much of Aquinas' concern with death centers around the condition of the soul after death. Since, "it is...contrary to the nature of the soul to be without a body," the resurrection is seen in a particularly favorable light. The resurrection is for Aquinas philosophically sound since the goal of man is happiness and happiness is impossible without a body both in this natural world and in the world to come. Therefore "perfect happiness must await a future state in which body and soul will be reunited." Moreover punishment for men's sins also necessitates a reunion of soul and body. Thus a resurrection is required. "In his risen and glorified state, or in his damned state, man will be immortal, animal, and incorruptible." (quoted in Gatch, 60) Since the soul must be purified before it reaches perfection penance became a necessity of the soul's journey. The final ratification of the soul's condition at the end of that journey comes at the Last Judgment. Aquinas, in exemplary medieval fashion, synthesizes philosophical, biblical, and ecclesiological aspects of the problem of death.

Classical Protestant Reformers— Martin Luther and John Calvin

Theologically the classical Protestant Reformers of the sixteenth century remained men of the medieval world in their intellectual emphases. However, culturally the Reformation was parallel to and a specific facet of the Renaissance and thus a break with the medieval world.

Martin Luther and John Calvin both saw God as Absolute Sovereign based on the paradigm of the medieval king. Their focus was on scripture rather than on classical Greek thought. This present earthly life was to be lived for the sake of the world to come. Their zeal for reform of the church climaxed a process which had been struggling to make a difference for centuries. Eventually it would result in a break with the Roman Catholic Church rather than a re-formation of it. They repudiated the Thomistic, or Scholastic, approach which had been the basis of Catholic theology from the 13th century on and would continue to dominate until into the 20th century. It stressed the seven sacraments clearly reaffirmed by the Council of Trent in the 16th century. Included in the sanctioned beliefs of the Church was the doctrine of purgatory. Contrasted with Roman Catholicism's seven sacraments were the two sacraments accepted by both Luther and Calvin. Baptism and the Lord's Supper were considered on a par with the preaching of the Word. Their definition of the church was "where the Word is rightly preached and the sacraments duly administered." It was Luther's reaction to purgatory by way of his attack on penance and the sale of indulgences which led to consideration of the problem of death for him. Life in this world is a preparation for the world to come. This is the only acceptable purgation for the Christian. Luther having considered reason "a damned whore" left the question of the immortality of the soul for the philosophers. Since salvation came from grace alone through scripture alone by faith alone it was enough to believe in the biblical affirmation of the resurrection and last judgment without mapping the terrain.

Another aspect of Luther should be kept in mind. In an existential vein Luther reminded his hearers that since every person must die for himself every one must know what he believes for himself. The priesthood of believers was an antidote to death in that having trusted in Christ for his salvation a person's fate after death could be left to the just God who sacrificed himself through Christ for the elect's salvation. Christians were to be Christ to one another and in their death as in their life bear witness to the all sufficient saving power of God through Christ.

John Calvin shared Luther's Christological center but spoke more directly than Luther of the immortality of the soul. It is the soul which is the "proper seat of the image of God." Like Luther, Calvin believed the elaboration of this doctrine was more properly philosophical than theological. Also like Luther, Calvin rejected the medieval doctrine of purgatory and turned to the more individualistic relationship of the Christian to God through Christ. Salvation is the work of the sovereign God through Christ, it is not a work in which the church is efficacious. Only by God's grace is any one saved. Justice demands that since all persons are sinners all should receive their just desserts, i.e. punishment after death for their sins. Again as for Luther, this life is a purging of sins without assurance that the soul will be prepared for the life to come after death. The elect, however, enjoy immortality after death. For Calvin, the resurrection at the last is the final seal of God's election of some to life eternal and the just condemnation of others to a state of endless perdition.

John Wesley and the English Evangelical Revival

William Cannon has observed, "Like Augustine and Luther before him, he [Wesley] was content merely to express his thoughts as occasions demanded." (7) The cultural context of the 18th century was different than that of the 5th, 13th or 16th century. The impact of the Renaissance was increasingly felt in the rise of the industrial revolution, the emergence of the age of reason or Enlightenment stressing individual rights, and the embryonic struggles of science and technology impacting on religion. Christianity felt the weight of rationalistic reactions against the excesses of religious fanaticism and warfare which had been all too prevalent. Political nationalism found its counterpart in the rise of national or established churches on the European continent and in England.

Thomas Cranmer the architect of the English Reformation formulated the Articles of Religion of the Anglican Church and developed the *Book of Common Prayer* with its oft quoted phrase, "in the midst of life we are in death." John Wesley before his "heart was strangely warmed" was an Anglican priest who at Oxford experienced dissatisfaction with an excessive emphasis on reason and distrust of emotion in religion prevalent in the church he served. Jeremy Taylor's *Rules and Exercises of Holy Living and Holy Dying* made a profound impact on the fearful young Wesley. This work was in the background of his thought in the tumultuous sea voyage as he sailed toward Savannah, Georgia to take up his ministry in the new world. The simple piety and sustaining faith of the Moravians aboard ship in the midst of a violent storm and the imminent threat of death stirred him deeply. As Wesley matured theologically he came to hold firmly to the conviction that Christ offers to all who will accept it a way of life in which men and women are forgiven of their sins and justified before God. Such justification leads, as it had for Luther, to doing works of love. God's continuing presence equips the Christian for a life of holiness leading to sanctification. "Christian perfection" releases a person from the bondage of sin and the fear of death which Wesley saw as the "consummate penalty of sin." (Cannon 196)

Wesley's conviction of man's struggle with sin and its consequences in death was to have pervasive influence on American frontier religious life. For many Americans, as for Wesley, the Kingdom of God was both a present reality and a fullness yet to come after death. The Christian life was "as a pilgrim way, with this present time as a time of decision and preparation for the final life of the kingdom still to come." (Williams 192) While the Kingdom of God was already a present reality into which one entered, it was even more an eschatological expectation. This duality was matched by another—personal or inward religion and social or outward religion. Death would be followed by

> the judgment, following the general resurrection, at which Christ shall separate the righteous from the unrighteous, with the righteous inheriting eternal life and the unrighteous being delivered into the everlasting punishment of hell. (Williams 198)

For Wesley the emphasis was on God's grace in Christ as the way beyond death, judgment, and punishment to eternal life in God for all those who in true repentance accepted it.

A few 20th century theological perspectives

The closer we come to our own time the more difficult the task becomes of selecting representative theological voices. Each of us holds to some theologians more dearly than to others, often for the assistance they have been to us personally. To omit theologians like Karl Barth, Emil Brunner, Nels F.S. Ferre, or Reinhold and Richard Niebuhr is difficult to defend. Nevertheless, we are limiting ourselves here to the views of Nicholas Berdyaev, Paul Tillich, Helmut Thielicke, Franz Rosenzweig, and Karl Rahner. In them we receive the insights of a philosopher of religion, a philosophical theologian, a pastoral theologian, a Jewish religious thinker, and an influential Catholic theologian.

Nicholas Berdyaev was an unorthodox Russian Orthodox thinker, captivated by freedom and exiled from Russia in 1925. The Russian Orthodox heritage, the long history of western mysticism, and the subjectivistic philosophy of existentialism interacted in his thought. Man, whose life is both a gift and an achievement, is co-creator with God of his destiny. The personality which has fully realized itself freeing itself from the enslavement of this world cannot die for it has attained the existence it was given. The tragedy of death for Berdyaev is that man refuses to exercise his creative freedom and realize his personality. Death is ambivalent for Berdyaev. It is an evil because it is the objectification by which the natural world dominates man as a thing. It further severs man from all temporal relationships which have had meaning for him. It singles a person out to judge whether his or her existence has become theandric (God/man; divine/human) or has remained merely natural. On the other hand, death is for Berdyaev the light of eternity where time has given way to the qualitative infinity of spirit. (Lowrie 271)

For Berdyaev the resurrection is the Christian answer to death but the resurrection is a mystical event in which theandric existence affirms that love is stronger than death so that no personal relationship is finally subject to death's destructive power. (333)

Taking Berdyaev seriously helps prevent our settling for a single, unalterable, and conclusive answer to ultimate questions. A careful reading of Berdyaev's works enables us to appreciate death as a mystery with moral imperatives. Since every person lives under the prospect of indeterminate death, men and women should treat the living so as to aid in freeing them for creative personal fulfillment with the awareness of our common end in death.

Paul Tillich had a greater influence on twentieth-century theology than any other theologian, with the possible exception of Karl Barth. Tillich sought to make Christian theology relevant in 20th century culture. In 1933 it became impossible for him to continue his work in Nazi Germany so he came to America teaching, speaking, and writing at numerous major universities before his death in 1965. Even though his insights had profound impact on Christian theology some considered his theology heretical in the same way centuries earlier the creative philosophical theologian Origen had been deemed a heretic.

Tillich's theological method uses two foci—the acceptance of the theological circle and the method of correlation. The circularity of faith leads to the realization that every theological problem demands recognition and treatment of other problems; to deal with death one must also treat creation, salvation, and so forth. The ontological metaphysic in which being returns to itself in spite of non-being is not the same picture of reality as the biblical drama in which God is working His purposes out in the actions of human beings. However, Tillich considers these positions reconcilable.[4] Freedom and decision are human necessities for both the Jewish biblical approach and the Greek philosophical one. At its simplest the method of correlation has philosophy posing the questions to which theology proffers answers. Tillich uses the Greek categories of being and non-being rather than the Jewish categories of life and death. Tillich urges human beings to go "beyond"—beyond Jesus the Christ to the New Being, beyond the God of theism to the Ground of Being itself. Tillich's theology has been of help to intellectual readers who seek to come to grips with the problem of death as is noted in the account of "a brilliant young man who with a fatal disease spent his last months reading *The Shaking of the Foundations* and found insight into the meaning of the Christian faith for one facing death". (Kegley and Bretall, xi)

Human beings live in a boundary situation of unrest, insecurity, anxiety or "the state in which a being is aware of its possible non-being." (Tillich, *The Courage to Be,* 35) The answer to death, as to despair, is in the courage to be which accepts finitude in spite of its contingency. This acceptance leads to participation in eternal life or communion with God. Such communion brings reunion of man with the depth and ground of being. The Christian finds this new being in Jesus whom man recognizes as the Christ because he has experienced the new being in himself. It is not the New Being in Jesus as the Christ which is emphasized so much as our experience of New Being which becomes intelligible to us by the New Testament picture of Jesus as the Christ. The divine love which a man or woman experiences in the depths of his or her being has manifested itself in the New Being of Jesus as the Christ who has shown the ultimate strength of love over death. For Tillich life in the Spirit as participation in the eternal is the answer to death. ("The Eternal Now" 38)

Tillich uses two constellations of symbols for this universal religious concept—the mystic and the prophetic-religious. While the mystic is most emphatic in Eastern religions, it is not limited to them. Western religions—Judaism, Christianity, and Islam—have symbolized eternal life in the prophetic-religious which includes both the immortality of the soul and the resurrection of the body.[5] Tillich agrees that resurrection is "the central Christian symbol" (*Systematic Theology*, Vol. 2, 157)

To these two primary symbols a third symbol is added. It is the Kingdom of God, an order of justice in ultimate fulfillment where the individual is not lost but is fulfilled according to the realized potentialities of his being and perfection.[6] The Kingdom of God is the completion of all other symbols of Eternal Life for in it participation and individualization are brought together in universal fulfillment. Here we compare Arnold Toynbee's observation:

> The similarity of the findings of modern Western psychologists, Hindu philosophers, and mystics of many schools point to an answer to the riddle of the sequel to death. These findings suggest that death's sequel is neither annihilation nor personal immortality, but is a re-merger in an ultimate Spiritual Reality from which the human personality that lives and dies has temporarily detached itself by a tour de force—purchasing a partial independence from its source at the cost of a partial alienation from it. (182)

Helmut Thielicke has repeatedly explored the theme of death. Among his early major works was *Tod und Leben: Studien zur Christlichen Anthropologie* (1946), which appeared in an English translation in 1970. When his colleagues at the University of Hamburg honored him with a festschrift on his sixtieth birthday they chose the motif of death and life and the title *Leben Angesichts des Todes: Beitrage zum theologischen Problem des Todes.*[7]

Martin Marty said of Thielicke, "few are his peers for synthesizing respectable scholarly inquiry and informed practical churchmanship."[8] The theologian's concern is with what God is saying to man in the most universal of human experiences—death. Death is a problem of personal relationship of man to

God for it discloses man's end-purpose in life and shatters the illusions by which man seeks to shield himself from its reality.

Human beings have both a nature and a history. As part of nature we move toward biological death, but having a history which we create and fashion in personal relationship with God and other human beings that death inevitably takes on new meaning. History is the sphere of the uniquely individual or personal rather than the impersonal, duplicatable, and interchangable. A person's history begins in God's call to him and in that person's response as he exercises his freedom toward God. The denial of such relationship leaves human beings with a "being toward death", a concept essential to the thought of Martin Heidegger.[9] In attempting to escape from the reality of his death man submerges himself in the impersonal mass and trades his authentic personal life for the inauthentic role of a functionary. He functions, for instance, as a biological, economic, political, professional cipher in the mass of humanity. In his personal being a man may turn away from the natural to the historical in which the distorted image of God in him is restored in Christ. Here he accepts his life as having an end-purpose. Having separated from God in the guilt and disobedience of sin, he is brought anew to a trusting relationship with God. Having lived in his solitariness seeking to be his own god, he turns to accept himself as created in the image of God and meant for community.

Death is judgment making the fate of one's life known. Its message is either one of solitariness or community, of a forfeited relationship or a fulfilled one.

Thielicke follows Luther, and before him Athanasius, in pursuit of a Christian answer to death in speaking of relationship of man with Jesus the Christ: "He makes our death to be his and his death to be ours." (*The Silence of God*, 86) The sign and seal of this transaction is the resurrection. Jesus Christ who really died was raised from death in a conquest of death by which death is de-powered in a decisive defeat though its existence continues until the Last Judgment. In a position reminiscent of Soren Kierkegaard, Thielicke sees the resurrection as the sign apprehended in discipleship rather than known in the veracity of historical scholarship. It is found in a personal relation in which God raises man after death's destructive power has accomplished its work. Christ is the Christian's companion and "elder brother" in whose company one walks "through the shadows which stretch over all of life and are darkest in death." (*Christ and the Meaning of Life,* 138)

Franz Rosenzweig, a remarkable Jewish interpreter of death and its meaning, wrote "each fearfully anticipates the day when he must make the journey into the dark." (Glatzer, 180) This earthly fear is life-long for death is an "inexorable *something* that can't be got rid of." (Glatzer 182) Rosenzweig expresses and exemplifies a profoundly personal religious commitment— openness to God in the present rather than a slavish adherence to the "fixity of a religious institution." (Glatzer, 203)

This openness to God, to life itself, is as fearful as death. Some human beings "would rather not live, if living means dying." (Glatzer, 211) The daily monotony of disappointments and failures belong to death making it difficult to come to the acceptance that "being able to live means being compelled to die." (Glatzer, 212) Once acceptance is made, a man or woman is free toward the open and unknown future. "There is no cure for death. Not even health. But the healthy man has the strength to walk alive to his grave." (Glatzer, 213)

As Nahum Glatzer has pointed out in his biography of Rosenzweig life was for him "Jewish life" drawn from its spiritual heritage and made intensely, personally his own:

> The greatest test was the eight years of paralysis. Here 'life' meant enduring with an upright spirit pain, physical privation, and gradual decline of the strength to life; it meant filling every day with spirit; with help and counsel to family, friends, and the community at large; and with a healthy sense of humor. All this in preparation for the great day of death which was to be accepted in faith and in freedom. (xxxiii)

Herman E. Schaalman points out how relevant Rosenzweig's treatment of death can be:

> Rosenzweig offers an alternative to both the self-annihilating conclusion of idealism and the well-nigh solipsistic consequence of existentialism. By living 'before

God', i.e. in his presence and in response to him and the others, the human community, man falls victim neither to the paralysis of generality nor to the corrosion of absurdity. In understanding himself to be loved, man becomes capable of life and thus comes to share life and eternity...The most obvious merit of that thought is that it is a structure, a cohesive account of traditional Jewish thought and a teaching couched in the language of the twentieth century, combining the method of absolute empiricism with the most subtle and sensitive understanding of Torah and rabbinic sources. One would perhaps have to go back as far as Maimonides' *The Guide to the Perplexed* to find another such comprehensively structured statement of Jewish belief. (235)

Karl Rahner, as a result of his involvement in the Second Vatican Council, 1962–1965, emerged to a wider public than his own Roman Catholicism. Pope John XXIII convened the Council to let the refreshing winds of the Holy Spirit blow through the Vatican but did not live to see its completion. Rahner is a prolific and complex theologian who has often contended that an adequate theology of death is necessary if we are to understand and appreciate the significance of the death of Christ. In *On the Theology of Death* he approaches death as "an event", as "the effect of sin" and as "a participation in Christ's death."[10]

Human death is the death of the whole person for which Christian theology uses both the term "immortality of the soul" and "resurrection of the flesh." Life after death is eternal life in a new dimension not a mere extension of life as it is now lived, "...the theology of St. John makes it clear that the existence of eternity grows out of time and is not merely the afterthought of a reward appended to time."[11]

As Rahner sees it, in death the soul is separated from the body and attains a universal relationship to the whole material world. It also is in purgatory expiating the remains of past sins. Death ends man's earthly pilgrimage and sets his destiny.

Rahner points out that it is no longer possible for one's personal development and relationship to God to change, since "at the moment of death the personal relation of a man to God becomes fixed for all eternity.... Death, therefore, can be nothing else than the culminating personal act of the soul's temporal development, that act by which it brings its life in time to a definitive peak of personal perfection. (Gelpi, 23) Death is both a physical end and a spiritual culmination: "not a mere biological event" but "a completely human event." (Roberts 252)

A person's death can be either the guilty death of a man or woman as sinner or the redeemed death in grace in Christ. It is an ambiguous event obscured as a consequence of sin. Such ambiguity forces human beings to a decision either to trust their lives and deaths into God's hands or die 'a death of despair and unreality." (Gelpi, 25) The fear of death, so much a part of human existence, is itself a result of the power of sin. "In death, man's personal freedom is engaged wholly as never before. The final act of freedom completes and summarizes the series of human free acts in a choice recapitulating in a sense, all of life's choices. (Roberts 254)

Christ's death is, "that definitive personal act by which he sums up, seals, and lovingly offers to his Father the whole of his life and being in propitiation for mankind." (Gelpi, 26) The resurrection of Christ is God's acceptance of this offering of death for mankind. The Christian is baptized into the death of Christ and by this symbolic death accepts the seal of death to his sin. The Eucharist is the continual communal experience which makes Christ's death present to us. In addition to the two sacraments of baptism and the Eucharist, the sacramental anointing of the sick "either restores the sick man to health or grants him the grace of a death in Christ." (Gelpi, 28)

Over against moral, cultic, or mystical asceticism Rahner advocates Christian asceticism which is

> essentially a participation in the passion and death of Christ....Christian asceticism is essentially the anticipatory acceptance of death in faith through suffering....
> But most of all, the death of Christ transforms the Christian act of dying. Though they resemble one another empirically, the death of a Christian is essentially different from the death of a sinner. For the Christian, death is no longer a punishment for sin, but only a

consequence of it ....In death the Christian experiences the consequences of sin, the darkness and bitterness of separation from God. But in the midst of it all he believes and hopes in the divine mercy and lovingly abandons himself wholly into the hands of his heavenly father. (Gelpi, 29–30)

We have looked briefly at some theological reflections on death. The diversity could be matched by treatments in art, drama, literature, philosophy, psychology, sociology, music, or most any area of human concern. As the intellectual and cultural climate changes the theological emphases and categories reflect those thematic changes. Making sense of life and death must be done afresh every time those changes come about. There are always some voices more influential than others, some more iconoclastic, some more tied to the past, some more radically adrift.

The theologians we have glanced at expressed the prevailing motifs of their time. The more extreme and alienated voices for whom the death of God announced by Friedrich Nietzsche in the 19th century and adumbrated by mid-20th century theologians did not bring the hoped-for elevation of man. Instead they led to human despair. I have chosen not to include these. Nor did I include those theologians whose tenacity to the faith once and forever delivered to the saints offered nothing new or creative. In the continuum of those presented in this chapter we have glimpsed the central stresses of our time. Men and women facing death must live life in personal freedom and responsibility. This places the focus on the cruciality of each person's experience of relationship "without God," "before God," or "with God". The decisive process of living one's own life and dying one's own death both demands and calls forth human integrity and dignity.

[1] See Karl Rahner, "On Martyrdom," *On the Theology of Death* (1961). Trans. Charles H. Henkey. pp. 89–127.
[2] See Charles Biggs. *The Christian Platonists of Alexandria* (1886).
[3] For a full discussion of this matter see the *Writings of Saint Augustine Volume 2.* "St. Augustine: Immortality of the Soul and Other Works. *The Fathers of the Church a New Translation* (1947).

[4]Paul Tillich. *Biblical Religion and the Search for Ultimate Reality* (1955).

[5]Paul Tillich, "Symbols of Eternal Life," *Harvard Divinity Bulletin*, 6 (April 1962): pp.1–10.

[6]See Tillich, *Systematic Theology*. Vol. 3 (1963), pp 406–409.

[7]Published by Mohr (Siebeck) of Tubingen in 1968.

[8]In the introduction to Thielicke, *A Little Exercise for Young Theologians* (1962). page viii.

[9]Martin Heidegger, *Being and Time* (1962). Trans. John Macquarrie and Edward Robinson.

[10]Rahner, *On the Theology of Death* (1961).

[11]Henry J. Cargas and Ann White, eds.. *Death and Hope* (1971).

Chapter 5

Actively and Passively Coping with Death

Everyone dies; everyone has some means of coping with death. In part this is a cultural matter as Robert Fulton points out

> Every society of men has its own distinct culture. Although death is the lot of all men, each society copes with death in terms of its own set of ideas, beliefs, values and practices. Some societies, for instance, see death as inevitable and an improvement in one's prospects and status. Others do not. Mourning or weeping over the loss of an individual is not everywhere considered appropriate behavior. (103)

Coping is a means of attempting to solve the problem, but since death is a mystery rather than a problem, it is insoluble. We cope with death without eliminating its mystery.

There are innumerable ways of coping. Arnold Toynbee uses several categories to discuss coping with death: hedonism, pessimism, attempts to circumvent death by physical counter-measures, attempts to circumvent death by winning fame, self-liberation from self-centeredness by putting one's treasure in future generations of one's fellow human beings, self-liberation from self-centeredness by merging oneself in ultimate reality, the belief in the personal immortality of human souls, the belief in the resurrection of human bodies, and the hope of heaven and the fear of hell. (59–94)

In this chapter we look at coping with death in terms of passive and active categories. Passive is a descriptive not a pejorative term in the sense that a person turns away from death and backs into it, so to speak, letting it happen to him or her. Passive coping is not a single unified human experience. It may be understood as a person's attempt to ignore, deny, or resign oneself to death. Each of these ways carries different meanings with it. Active coping, on the other hand, seeks to preserve the freedom and integrity of each person facing death by confronting or meeting the reality of the event and the personal and interpersonal significance of its meaning. Active coping is also not a single experience but has varied forms which seek to face, affirm, or accept death as a basic human value.

Passive means of coping with death

We tend to ignore whatever we believe doesn't have value for us and are indifferent to whatever we consider inconsequential. We do not ignore anything we consider essential for our well being or for attaining our objectives. Any one who wishes to live off the land in isolation from others can ignore the formalities of higher education which are prerequisite to becoming a doctor, lawyer, teacher or other professional. He cannot ignore the necessity of learning how to cope with the environment in which he lives. He must learn to hunt or gather, to plant or forage. The content and form learning takes is conditioned by the objectives the learner considers worthwhile. The would-be hermit ignores as a matter of indifference for him the restrictions of prolonged formal education which the would-be professional person accepts as legitimate. Neither of them can ignore learning itself and survive.

Someone may consider death of little consequence to her life. But, in actuality she copes with it by ignoring it or treating it with indifference until it comes into the range of her immediate experience where the factual event necessitates a meaning. It can then no longer be ignored. Ignoring death may be effective for a person so long as she is not faced with the death of someone who has special value for her, someone who cannot be regarded with indifference. She may let the deaths of the faceless masses of society pass her by without notice. But, it is a distinctive characteristic of being human to value particular persons and have feelings for their life. In the abstract it may be a convincing argument to ignore death in general in much the same way one ignores other aspects of the human experience. However, in the particular event of one's own death or the death of one whose life is highly prized the argument becomes vacuous:

I could not be bothered with death,
Ignored its insatiable devouring;
Til long submerged it surfaced,
Drowning laughter with sorrow,
Indifference with care.

Ignoring death is a means of coping. In the long run, however, it must be transferred to some form of active coping in the demanding situation of the death of a person whose life is dear.

Denial is another passive means of coping with death. It is an act of repudiation rather than of indifference which is the primary mode of ignoring death. Death is passed by until it becomes impassible. Confronted with it either in the event it self or anticipatorily, one refuses to admit death has human consequences and considers it to have no reality. Severe and prolonged denial is characteristic of a psychotic or neurotic personality whose fantasy world will not admit impingement by any kind of threatening reality. As Mervyn Shoor and Mary Speed point out,

> When it [death and the mourning process that follows] is not integrated it may become so pathological, so distorted, that it may not even be recognizable as a variant of the mourning process. In adults these variant reactions may take the form of alcoholism, mental illness, depressive states, obesity, or various neurotic manifestations. (201)

An experience early in life of emotional deprivation may have been so traumatic as to render a person unable to cope with further loss and separation of the death of a loved one. Its reality is met by denial which has been the long-standing means of coping for that person. This is a form of coping, a passive way of integrating death into that person's approach to life.

Adolph Christ did a study of 100 psychiatric patients over sixty years of age at a San Francisco general hospital in 1959. His findings are still worth considering:

> 87% stated they had never talked about death or dying before. One can speculate that at least some of their psychiatric symptoms, which often included fear of being poisoned, killed, or thrown out of their homes, as well as frank, somatic delusions, may be symptoms of marked denial of death. (152)

Denial may be the means of coping, not only for the acutely mentally ill who live in the pretense that death has not occurred nor will occur, but for others as well. Those who attribute reality only to a spiritual realm and consider their existence in the here and now of time and space, flesh and blood, a transitory sentence not affecting their real life are engaging in a form of coping by denial. Death is treated as only a sleep. It is for them but a temporary incursion into the real world of the life of mind and spirit which transcends the realm of the body to which one has been confined and condemned.

> *Death—there is no death,*
> *Only liberation from life's necessity or demand;*
> *Death must be denied by life set free.*
> *Alas, we still die.*

Death is denied as of little consequence in the same way that the meanings of other events of life have been denied because they were inseparable from physical existence.

Resignation is a third passive means of coping. Resignation is the middle way of passivity between ignoring and denial. Here a person surrenders to the reality of death as inevitable. Standing powerless before it and seeing no hope beyond it the resigned person simply submits to it seeking to incorporate it into his context of reality. This may appear an affirmation of the facticity of death as a meaningless experience to which one can accommodate himself by resignation. However, the act of resignation is itself the meaning assigned to death. Even this attempt at treating death simply as an objective fact devoid of meaning turns out to be a way of attributing meaning to it.

Weave Fates your patterned tapestry,
This underside of tangled ends and twisted cords;
Weave death into a riddled scheme,
Resigned to riddles, rages, ruin we cease to be.

If a person dies as he has lived and his life has been a resignation of himself to events to which he believes he was subjected beyond his control, it is to be expected that the final act of his life would be resignation.

Active means of coping with death

The active cluster of means of coping with death includes facing, affirming, and accepting death. These are the opposites of the passive forms of ignoring, denying, and resignation before the encounter with death.

Facing death is the active counterpart of ignoring which treats death with indifference since it is considered of little value. In facing death one acknowledges that it can not be treated with indifference. James Kavanaugh has developed this approach in his book *Facing Death*. In the end a person has to come face-to-face with death. To do so requires an amount of courage lacking in ignoring it. Facing death goes beyond ignoring, denying or resigning oneself to its reality and inevitability. A person in facing death commits himself to dying a good death. Throughout life he has faced other uncertain or unanticipated significant events. Now he is confident that his involvement with death will not be inconsistent with his reactions to life. Having lived his own life he is now ready to face his own death. Paul Irion reminds us, "The contemplation of death provides something of the quality of our living, and the meaningful regard for our living is preparation for dying. This needs to be seen in more than moralistic terms." (110) A person who has faced life accounting for herself in a meaningful manner now anticipates facing her own death or the death of her loved ones confident that the resources necessary for acquitting herself properly will be sufficient.

Death will not make a mockery of life;
No mask will hide the face from fear or pain.
Face to face its dehumanizing force must yield its power;
Powerless to indignify my ending and my end.

Death may also be coped with by affirming it. Instead of avoidance by denial, affirmation of death runs headlong to meet it considering it the greatest good. Many persons of different religious and philosophical persuasions have grown rhapsodic over their approaching death. "Come sweet death" anticipates a value in excess of anything experienced in this life. It may be that the conditions of life have been such as to deprive a person of the essentials requisite for a good life. Oppression, torture, poverty, slavery, dehumanization can elicit a conviction that death is preferable to a life without a conceivable future superior to the one now being experienced. Even the possibility of extinction or annihilation holds less terror than the indefinite continuation of a life which carries little significance. The affirmation of death may be based on the belief that what follows death will be of such inestimable value that this life by comparison is worthless.

The extreme of affirming death is seen in a martyr provoking his own death. Martyrdom may be ritually acceptable suicide, but since one is presumed not to inflict death on himself it does not carry the condemnation which suicide normally has borne. In fact, in Roman Catholic theology while suicide is not sanctioned even denying the suicide burial in a sanctified cemetery, martyrdom is viewed as the most blessed of deaths assuring the faithful an immediate access to paradise. Islam's position is virtually the same.

How ironic that the Crusades pitted Christians and Muslims against each other in the name of God with both sides assuring their warriors that a heroic death in destroying the infidel would bring with it immediate access to paradise. Very early in the life of the church men and women were bolstered in their encounter with death by a vision of the glories of superior life with their Lord after death.

> *Come vanquishing death and be vanquished!*
> *My life I give up, to take again*
> *When having served its purpose*
> *Its Rightful Owner receives it purified.*

Religious history is filled with incidents of ordinary believers who consider death the persecutor seeking to destroy them. They are convinced that death itself is defeated by God. By God's re-creatively victorious act, death has been made the passageway to true life beyond death. Franz Borkenau even states, "defiance of death is at the core of the Christian message." (51)

Death is further coped with by deliberate acceptance. Resignation signifies submission because of an inability to control an event. Sometimes hopelessness and futility result. Acceptance, on the other hand, recognizes the reality of death including its inevitable separation but integrates it into the context of life. Robert Neale in his book *The Art of Dying* sets forth several approaches to death and dying with concrete means of meeting and accepting it. Death becomes a revelatory experience casting light on the history and future of the dying person and those related to her. One accepts it without the tempting nonchalance of merely facing it or the abandonment of the death-affirmer who makes it his primary life-value. The person accepting death recognizes the duality of the situation: relationships and events which have supported him and aided in forming his identity, such as his family, work, or creativity will now be severed from him as he will be finally or permanently separated from them. In spite of this, he has integrated the event into his life so that death is not alien to life's purpose of fulfillment. As Paul Irion sees it:

> The dying person is helped to confront the meaning of what is transpiring in his experience within the context of the meaning of his entire life. A new honesty and authenticity develops which does not avoid death but rather enables the person to die with the dignity of meaning. (39)

This integration may have come about by a religious faith which sees death as the entrance to new dimensions of life. Or it may have been arrived at through a naturalistic position of the necessity of all energy having in time to change its form. In either case, death is accepted as no longer a threat to the dignity and purposefulness of a person's humanity or an obliteration of the value of his having lived.

I would not leave if staying would fulfill the dreams;
The loneliness, loss, and empty nights I cannot fill.
Biographies have their end as their beginning.
Life-lived must take into itself death-died.

Philosophical and cultural support systems for coping with death

Religion serves as a major means of coping with death. It is not, however, the only one. My own experience over a lifetime confirms my belief that generally men and women die like they live. If religion has been an important part of their lives before the last stage of the journey it continues to be so often intensifying. If religion has not been that important they do not all of a sudden become religious as they face death. There are, however, incidents in which sudden conversions take place and religion or faith becomes all important as a person walks toward death.

In the light of the passive and active categories we have looked at religion has little to offer persons adopting a passive approach. If a person adopts a posture toward death which allows him or her to ignore, deny, or resign himself to death there is little support religion can offer. Philosophical or cultural support systems then take on religion's functions.

A prevalent approach in our scientifically oriented age sees death from a naturalistic vantage point. This appears to be the most often expressed outlook for those persons who do not find religion their main support. A scientific worldview predisposes human beings to a predilection for empirical verification and the materialistic reductionism this may entail. If the only truth of any real value is empirically verifiable truth, then the obvious conclusion is that death is simply that a material being has ceased to function. It then moves to the dissolution of its form and the transposition of its energy into other forms of mass. Human beings identified with the animal realm of which they are a part are subject to the same ending as all organic life. All elements of nature whether plants or animals die. It is natural to accept a human's death as another example of the universal condition. Death is the cessation of those functions which mark men and women as alive. Having come from dust we return to dust. That is the end of the matter. Though this view does not necessarily devalue life, it may lead a person to believe that there really is no meaning beyond survival. Staying alive as long as possible becomes the prime objective. Simple longevity rather than the qualitative development of one's life sets the priorities. This view has tremendous implications for the current astronomical costs of health care when the overriding objective is to keep a person alive at any cost and by any means for as long as possible without regard to the quality of life being sustained. If physical survival is the only acceptable value death makes no sense. Consequently, prolonging material existence is the only meaningful end. Sometimes even if a person has reconciled himself to his death, especially after an extended illness, those around him including some medical personnel, may still hold to a naturalistic refusal to see death from any other vantage point and refuse to let him go without the invasive and artificial means being used to keep him "alive" by what are ironically known as heroic measures.

Jacques Choron notes that a naturalistic means of coping may lead to a conclusion of the worthlessness of human life:

> Then with apparently incontrovertible logic the conclusion imposes itself that if after a brief sojourn on this earth man is destined to leave it forever—sometimes suddenly, and often prematurely—and simply return to dust, life does not make sense. (162)

A man or woman may go kicking and screaming against his natural demise or he or she may go quietly into that black night, but like all nature which knows no permanence of form he or she too must pass away. No doubt some are reminded here of Dylan Thomas' advice to his father in the poem "Do not go gentle into that good night." But, for Thomas, as Amos Wilder has noted:

> All in all Dylan Thomas celebrates death-in-life in a neo-Romantic manner. What gives it a certain significance is his breaking away from a banal pantheism and his kinship to the apocalyptic or surrealist grasp of existence. (28–29)

In another of Thomas' poems, "Ceremony after a Fire Raid" the whole human race becomes the concern of the poet focused in "the cinder of the little skull."

This imagery reminded me of a hauntingly vivid impression made on me as a child. It was an experience I had while riding one Sunday afternoon with my family in a rural area of South Carolina near my home in Augusta, Georgia. We came upon the smoldering ruins of a sharecropper's house which had burned completely to the ground. My father parked the car on the side of the road. He and I joined the small group of helpless bystanders while my mother and sister waited in the car. Some men raked from the ashes the charred skull and skeleton of a young child and put them in a blanket one of the men had with him. Even when not seeking it death confronts us—even on a leisurely Sunday drive.

The romantic shares with the naturalist a profound admiration for nature but shifts the emphasis from nature's orderliness to its power. The romantic's favorite images are those in which the force of nature may be seen in the towering grandeur of the mountains, the surges of the sea, or the spectacle of a storm. Nature's individuality rather than its sameness is stressed. The particularity of the shell on the shore or the fruit on the tree is treasured not as another part of the whole the same as all the others, but as a part which uniquely has its own identity, though in a class with an infinite number of similar objects. The naturalistic approach stresses the sameness and orderliness of the whole; the romantic stresses the individuality, uniqueness, and capriciousness of the part. The fruit may drop from the tree and return again to the earth but it hung for a while in its separateness apart from all other fruits. A man may arise out of the stream of time only for a time. Ever so briefly he glistens in his own particularity which even death cannot take from him in that it cannot negate what he has been. As the Process Philosopher Charles Hartshorne picturesquely says it:

> Death is the last page of the last chapter of the book of one's life, as birth was the first page of the first chapter....Death cannot mean the destruction, or even the fading of the book of one's life; it can mean only the fixing of the concluding page. Death writes 'The End' upon the last page, but nothing further happens to the book, either by way of addition or subtraction. (102–103)

Moving further away from the natural and material is the mystical in which the great reality of being stretches beyond the individualized moment and encompasses all moments in itself. The mystic sees the simultaneity of all time in the eternality of the mystical experience. Since time and space are limited to this physical world, they are inappropriate categories for understanding the true nature of reality which subsumes time and space into itself. In the mystical experience there is only oneness. The drive to particularity important to the romantic is given up to the loss of the self in the One. All differentiations, including the line between time and eternity, are overcome. Death holds no power over such a reality, for death is a mark of a division between time and eternity. Like all other divisions, death is obliterated in the mystical experience which transcends them.

Something of the mystical is in the idealistic where the temporal and the spiritual are resolved. Reality lies in eternal ideas known to mind and are not subject to matter. The answer to death is in the affirmation that one's mind or soul is eternal or immortal. The soul is immune to the ravages of the material and mortal body. The mind transcends itself both backwards and forwards rather than being confined to the immediate present. Through memory and imagination the soul can remember where it has been and vicariously be where it is not. It is superior to the body which is finite, limited by both time and space. Death is the expected end to the limiting matter upon which the unlimited mind or soul has had to depend in this life. In death, the eternal mind or soul is set free from its material bounds.

Any notion of an aspect of man impervious to death may contribute more to the problem of human death than to a solution. Human life may be seen not as a form which inevitably must change or a particular element which must return to the whole, or an enlightenment overcoming all distinctions, or an element transcending the situation of life and death. Instead, human beings may be seen as the creators of their own life and the ones who must die their own deaths. Human death becomes categorically different than death in general. Each person's existential death is the death that matters most. Life is a being-towards-death in which one knows herself not as the fulfiller of a preconceived destiny but as the very creator of whatever destiny she fashions. Death may be an absurdity. If it is, then life is also absurd. Nothing a person does is able to prevent his death. Unlike animals forced to live the life given to them, human beings may make their own life. They must make their death their own if either life or death is to have meaning and save them from nothingness. Here is how Jose Ferrater Mora phrases it:

> Man is making himself constantly as man and that is what I meant by saying that he makes his own life. A certain biological structure and a number of psychological dispositions are in this respect necessary conditions. They are in no way merely contingent facts, purely circumstantial elements which man can take or leave as he pleases. A certain human body and a certain human mind are also a certain given man. Each man thus makes his own life with his body and mind, which are not solely 'things' but basic elements of man's existence. (158)

It is futile to make the pursuit of happiness the justification of one's existence when death is taken seriously. Life may be reduced to the pursuit of happiness but then death has to be assiduously forestalled since it is the final threat to happiness. For hedonism death cannot have an active role to play because death has nothing to contribute to one's happiness. Death may be ridiculed, scorned, made fun of, or ignored but can not be accepted or affirmed. It can be expected to bring only sadness and loss which happiness strives to destroy. Fiestas of death and festivals of defiant bravado in some cultures such as the Mexican observance of El Dia de las Muertos encourage happiness to flaunt itself in the face of death.

Before leaving this section and turning to religious approaches to coping with death we take note of Jacques Choron's "five modern answers to mortality":

"Eternal recurrence" in which man is a 'bridge'" (Nietzche)

"Life for others is the 'immortal' life" (Tolstoy)

"Faith in faith itself...in which despite everything we must believe in the beyond, in eternal life, and particularly the individual personal life." (Unamuno)

"Life and death are intimately bound up with each other and with the very essence of man." We must "ripen" into our death. (Rilke)

"death...makes the human condition 'unacceptable' for it reveals the absurdity, the nonsense of human life." (Malraux)[1]

There are many approaches to coping with death. I have pointed to only a few before turning to approaches from a religious perspective.

[1] For a full discussion of these answers see Choron, *Death and Modern Man* (1972) pp. 178–185.

Chapter 6

Coping with Death from a Religious Perspective

Religious approaches to coping with death

Religion is the most widely used means of coping with death. There is no single form since religion offers many approaches. From the beginning of human existence when human beings stood in awe of the mysterious realm of life ended in death, religion has provided humankind its foremost means of coping. A person does not have to fully agree with theories of the anthropologists Bronislaw Malinowski or Edward B. Tylor to acknowledge that religion arose as human beings sought to cope with the crises of their existence. In dance, mimetic drama, and rituals men and women sought means of responding to the mystery of the cessation of life. Where there had been another person whose life they had shared now there was only stillness and the void. In desperation, even before an intellectually sophisticated system of beliefs or theology was developed they acted out their despair, their inexplicable loss. They sought a way of recognizing the final separation and preserving the relationship which had given meaning to their own existence. Because they had the capacity to feel as well as to think they ritualized their grief long before they engaged in mental speculation on the event.

Could they accept so final a solution? It was not conceivable to them that something so primary as life could end so abruptly. They prepared the departed for a safe journey into the unknown while simultaneously protecting themselves and other living beings from the awesome power of discontented dead. Taboos of death became extensive and special means were devised for assuring the successful completion of this responsibility. Something of the primitive is still with modern men and women who seek appropriate disposal of the dead to allay their bewilderment in their living presence.

The global village concept has done much to strike down the provincialism of westerners who looked upon Eastern religions as pagan superstitions obstructing the true light of revealed religion. Awareness of the universality of religion as a basic human stance has helped in appreciating attempts of all religions to deal with primary human concerns. Eastern religions appear so complex as to encourage over-simplification in order to make them understandable with minimum effort and knowledge. They are lumped together as if there were only superficial differences between Hinduism, Buddhism, Confucianism, Shinto and others.

Recognizing their linear historical course helps us get a better grasp of Western religions. Judaism is understood in terms of biblical, rabbinical, and modern developments. Christianity is studied in terms of various segments such as the New Testament, patristics, Roman Catholicism, Eastern Orthodoxy and myriad branches of Protestantism. Historical awareness plays a major role in understanding Islam, particularly the struggles between Islam and Christianity and its internal struggles between Shias and Sunnis.

The cyclic context of Eastern religions causes us to sometimes treat them as monolithic structures impervious to the currents of time and place. Eastern religions, like Western religions, are dynamic processes, not static artifacts. They have their own life and speak with their own voice about crucial human problems.

Hinduism incorporates into itself an amazingly tolerant diversity which for the faithful poses no threat. However, to the polarized logic of a restrictive mind Hinduism appears filled with irreconcilable inconsistencies. Hinduism is able to take into itself the most sophisticated intellectuals as well as the most ignorant peasants. This has its parallel in Roman Catholicism where the most erudite Thomist may be found in the same fold as the Latin American peon whose faith doesn't raise the questions much less answer them which his co-religionist considers absolutely essential.

Death for the Hindu is a mystery as it is for all human beings. It is not a problem in the same way as for the westerner for whom life in time and space is set over against the life of eternity. Time is continuous and individuality is minimized by the doctrine of the transmigration of souls making this particular death but one of many which a person must die. The round of existences can stretch into billions of years before the soul returns to the World Soul from which it came. Momentarily, it is a spark from the great fire or a drop from the depth of the unfathomable ocean. This particular death cannot be the last enemy because life goes on. The faithfulness with which one lives out his life in the place he has been given in this round of existence is the crucial concern for it determines the direction which his or her soul takes in the next episode of its continuous journey.

Buddhism may be seen as a reform movement within Hinduism, but it is more appropriate to see it in its own right. Buddhism, at least in regards to Siddhartha Gautama, the Buddha, took a new look at death and its attendants—suffering and old age. Gautama sought some way of dealing with death to shorten the endless rounds of life and bring death to death. Nirvana was the return of the soul to the ineffable mystery of its origin where all contrarieties were overcome and passionless peace overcomes one's suffering and striving. The goal was to escape from suffering created and perpetuated by inordinate desire as one moved into the nothingness of not being.

Buddhism moved in two major directions. Theravada Buddhism held to a view that the arhat, or saint, should seek wisdom which would lead to Nirvana. Mahayana Buddhism developed in a variety of ways. One of the most prominent of these was to see the quest as a continuous act of compassion in which one's primary goal is to assist others in discovering their own buddha-nature in the journey toward nirvana. As an act of grace, those who find the secret of living and dying postpone their fulfillment in negation by returning as bodhisatvas to aid others in finding their way through life and death to Nirvana. Gautama apparently made no attempt to delineate the terrain of life after death; his followers could not resist the temptation. The Pure Land of Amitaba Buddhism offers a serenity and joy comparable to a Christian Heaven or Muslim Paradise. Buddhist doctrines of hell became as vigorously and graphically portrayed as the most fundamentalist Christian or Muslim pictures. A third branch of Buddhism, Vajrayana, set out to provide a guide through life and death with the *Tibetan Book of the Dead.* This gave death a more deliberately focused position. This branch is best known today because of the irrepressible affirmation of human values of love, joy, and peace eloquently spoken of and admirably lived out by the Dalai Lama. In Buddhism, as in other religions, there is no single response to death's mystery

Islam with its roots in Judaism and Christianity as well as in the animism of its native land and the influences of Persian and Eastern religions also affords means of coping with death. The faithful are promised a realm of delight and pleasure after death. All they have denied themselves in this life will be given to them in the life to come. The faithful Muslim makes his or her pilgrimage to Mecca as an act of devotion readying their soul for the journey into the life to come. Each Muslim is expected to engage in the greater jihad (spiritual struggle) by obediently submitting himself/herself completely to Allah. The conditions of the lesser jihad (holy war) are delineated in the Koran. Those who die in a holy war (jihad) are promised immediate access to heaven. As we noted earlier this belief of martyrdom as immediate access to heaven appeared very early in Christianity. It was ironically reemphasized in the call for Crusades against the Muslims who equaled that emphasis in jihad. On the other hand, the unfaithful or wicked faces a never-ending life of torment in hell as a judgment for his or her sin—again, a belief shared with many Christians.

Judaism has always taken death seriously. Men and women were created in the image of God. After the disobedience of Adam and Eve in the Garden of Eden, they were convinced that death was an ensuing judgment against them. Death's entrance into the human realm is tied into Adam and Eve's decision to stand over against God. Judaism was certain that God was God of all—death as well as life. Because of this, death had to be accounted for in relation to God. It was on the one hand the enemy of God and of mankind, while on the other hand, death at the end of a long and fruitful life was considered the natural end of life. Whatever happened to one after death was not the cause for despair or loss of hope. Biblical Judaism was convinced that life is lived in the security of God's hands. Even the shadowy existence beyond death was not beyond God's care.

Modern Judaism has no single view toward death. To some Jews, death is a naturalistic event concluding the human lifecycle and bringing about another form for matter. To others, death is a problem which has no solution. One asks as few questions as possible about it and practical annihilation is assumed. To still others, death ushers in a time of waiting for the coming of the Messiah when the Kingdom of God will be inaugurated on earth and the faithful dead will rule with him on a new earth. Some Jews see beyond death a time of judgment after which one goes either to a hell of punishment or a heaven of reward. Jewish thought is often erroneously stereotyped and restricted to a belief in death as the end with no continuation beyond. The intent of Judaism amidst its diversity has been to accept the reality of death and avoid escapism leading to delusion rather than to trust and hope.

Christianity has traditional approaches to coping with death. Ministry is invariably oriented toward dealing with death as the climactic crisis of human experience. The sacramental system of the Roman Catholic Church viewed from a humanistic perspective institutionalizes religious responses to the basic events of human life: birth (baptism), passage from childhood toward adulthood (confirmation), identification with the community (Eucharist), forgiveness and renewal (penance), personal relationships and identity (marriage or holy orders), and death (anointing of the sick, or as it was called before 1972 extreme unction or last rites). The priest functions as the solemnizer and authenticator of the profundity of the event in the divine depths of human experience. He stands as a symbol of hope and validation performing on behalf of another person the ritual which sets these experiences in a cosmic context of meaningfulness beyond the immediacy of the personal crisis. Death is accepted as personal with its meaning in the context of a system of belief posited on conviction of God's activity in creation.

Other expressions of the Christian faith do not carry the all-inclusive dimensions of integral involvement with culture. But, all religious approaches are dependent to an extent on the coinciding of belief and practice in the religious community and the recognition of the legitimacy of such beliefs and practices by the culture at large. For example, Southern Baptists have traditionally been supported by a Southern culture which while it may not have completely agreed with the beliefs and practices of the church at least sanctioned them as of positive value for a good community and urged their continuation as a kind of social cohesion.

The cultural situation of today is, of course, vastly different from Medieval Europe or even Protestant America in the 19th or 20th centuries. There is no longer the dominance of religious certification. America has not yet reached the stage of post-Christian Europe but the voluntarism and individualism which led to the proliferation of denominations has necessitated an increasing realization of religious pluralism. A pluralistic culture provides a more accepting attitude toward previously unknown religions as well as an option of rejecting any religious involvement.

Old ways have a habit of residually holding on long after deep personal participation has been abandoned. A minister is often called upon today to provide ministry to persons who have only a casual involvement with institutional religion but who wish religious ceremonies at the end. As we will note in the following section of this chapter, there is a need for some public recognition, not necessarily overtly religious, of a person having lived and subsequently having died.

For centuries Christianity's approach to death was marked by an emphasis on the finality of this finite life and a judgment at its end bringing with it either reward by entrance into heaven or condemnation to everlasting hell. This overwhelming prevalence has for the most part collapsed today. Yet, there are still practitioners in our society who hold steadfastly to this fear-centered approach. As a child growing up in Augusta, Georgia we lived a block away from a funeral home which had a chapel which was used not only for services for the dead but also religious meetings for the living, such as revivals. I remember going there to see a film depicting the horrors of a fiery hell and the exhortations to get saved and avoid this never-ending torment. The vivid colors of the roaring flames and the screams of the damned made a lasting impression on me. Many a night I went to sleep crying because some of my close relatives had not been saved and would be languishing in hell-fire for all eternity. I am sure my own religious progression was spurred on, in part, by a belief that there must be a better answer from Christianity for both the issues of life and death.

In Samuel Beckett's play *Endgame* the two characters Clov and Hamm are whiling away the time when Clov asks Hamm, "Do you believe in the life to come?" and Hamm responds cryptically, "Mine was always that." The life to come is no longer for most people a realm of terror or blissful reward, neither the celestial city nor the pit of fire so well known from Dante's *Inferno.* It is but an experience of the here and now which fails to satisfy before ending in the gaping hole of death,

Ministering in the face of death

What is a minister to do in such a situation if she is to provide an honest ministry to those coping with death? The first necessity is to start with the recognition of her own humanity which obviously entails the anticipation of her own death. Accepting one's own death is not only a religious, philosophical, and psychological concern, it is a practical matter as well. For everyone there are affairs to be put in order, arrangements to be made, persons to care for.

It is assumed that the minister, priest, or rabbi whose role frequently involves her in dealing with the dead and dying has come to grips with death as a personal event. This is not always the case.

Elisabeth Kubler-Ross, the pioneer in bringing death and dying out of the shadows and obscurity of a culture of denial into the light of honest appraisal, pointed out how ministers sometime become desensitized to death, "Only if we can learn to overcome our own fear can we truly help dying patients and then allow them to die with dignity and in peace and not avoid them and not yell at the peak of our voice, 'God is love,' until she drops dead."[1] During the late 1960s and 1970s Elisabeth Kubler-Ross spoke widely throughout the United States helping the general public come to grips with death and dying. I was privileged to be a part of a large audience of fascinated hearers for her presentations in Lexington, Kentucky. She was particularly eager that those in the caring professions of medicine and ministry learn better ways of coping with death. She reached even wider audiences through several television and video interview programs such as "Until I Die" (1970), "To Die Today" (1971)—a presentation of the Canadian Broadcasting Corporation, and "Just a Little Time" (1973). The Armed Forces was among those organizations availing themselves of her expertise in preparation of cassette tapes, workshops, and professional seminars such as "Ministering to the Terminally Ill".

The experience with death of some religious leaders has immunized them to its stark reality and inevitable shock. As bearers of comfort, peace, and hope that has allayed for others the sharpness of the separation, they may be led to the delusion that this can never happen to them. Often a personal encounter with death sets the whole matter in a new perspective.

I grew up in a culture where death was a part of life and children normally attended funeral services. My grandfather's body was brought to our home where his family and friends for a couple of days before the funeral service came to pay their last respects. But, it was not until the death of my first child who was born prematurely and lived twenty-three hours, that death became an insistent and painful reality. Walking through the valley of the shadow of death and feeling its agonizing presence made it a different reality. The fears and doubts were coupled with the separation and loss of anticipated joys making it an inescapable existential force. To have stared death in the face and found new faith and hope flowing out of the emptiness was to gain anew the divine love which sustains us in both life and death. It is to have moved from the position of a functionary who knows and does his job well in keeping with the demands before him to becoming a person who cannot push down the depth of his own humanity as he cares for others. Paul Irion says it well:

> Only as man acknowledges death as a part of life and faces his very own death does true authenticity come into his living. He learns in this way truly to care for others. He begins to appreciate the depth which is possible in the relationships of life. His life becomes filled with purposeful contributions to ongoing existence. (121)

It is possible to minister to the dying and their family without getting personally involved in a way similar to the actor who plays his part on the stage by following a method approach rather than entering into the character. Playing a part and taking on the persona of the character are two different things. Facing the anticipation of one's own death is a chance for honesty, to play one's part with integrity, in reaching the depths of one's own humanity.

It is certain that every one of us will die. The only uncertainty is when, and where, and how. Yet, some religious persons live as if they are special cases who, like Enoch, expect to be translated from earth to heaven without the intervention of death. Others use their piety as an excuse for their impracticality. God will take care of them and theirs when He calls them home. The problem is not so acute today as in times past when orphans often became the pitied objects of the church's and community's charity. Pension funds, insurance, and social security have given some respect and support to the fiscal necessities of family life under the threat of death. If provision has been made for the family's well-being in a sane and forthright manner, practical dimensions of the inevitability of one's death have been faced. Hopefully a will has been kept current, properly prepared and notarized and provisions made for the distribution of property. In addition to the will a letter of instruction for use at the time of death should prove helpful. It should include such matters as the location and intent of the will, location of valuable papers including insurance policies, instructions for funeral or memorial service, desires about the disposition of personal property not cared for explicitly in the will. An increasing number of persons are also making living wills, advance directives, or durable powers of attorney whereby they face the moral and social issues of their rights and responsibilities in dying a good death. These instruct physicians and other health care providers regarding one's wishes about extending one's life by artificial means or heroic measures when it is evident that death is imminent. It also can provide for the disposition of organs and of the body itself. Such foresight cannot take away the shock of one's death to a person's loved ones but it can minimize the strain and anxiety and give them a further sense of her thoughtfulness in caring for them. In the Epilogue I share my own attention to these matters.

I once attended a workshop conducted by Margie Jenkins and her husband "Jenks". It was the most exhilarating and informative experience I have had with the practical aspects of facing one's death in years of participation in such events. While you will not get the excitement of interaction with them from her book, *You Only Die Once* and its companion workbook, *You Only Die Once Personal Planner*, you will find in them the guidance and resources for taking the right steps to cope with the practical elements of your own death. Good, tasteful humor and personal experiences abound as she opens up new avenues while reaffirming the positive situations most persons have experienced in facing death and can readily identify with.

Coping with death through rites of passage

At this point of involvement with the dying the reality of one's theology of death becomes apparent. Even if up to now we have been able to keep our own death at arm's length we are finally forced by our face to face involvement with persons in the last stages of life's journey to consider the meanings of human life and death.

For many religious persons at or near the moment of death, a priest is desired to anoint the sick, to bring hope for the dying, and comfort to those closest to her. For most persons there is a desire to not die alone—to have someone with them in the final passing. It is not necessary that that person be an ordained clergyperson. In the sacredness of that passage the experience itself becomes holy.

A person is fortunate when he is privileged to die his own death, that is, a death consistent with the life he lived. Again I turn to my personal experiences; this time to the deaths of my father and mother. My father died quickly as a result of a heart attack at the age of 69. He had a major myocardial infarction at 42 but lived another 27 years. He had retired and sold his mechanical contracting business a few years prior to his fatal attack. On the day of his death he was working hard on a project in his yard as he had done on every project in his life. He had lived a good life giving generously back to the community and aiding numerous young people to continue their higher education. Death came quickly without prolonged agony or pain. His funeral was an outpouring of appreciation from many whom my sister and I had no idea he had helped. My mother, who preceded him in death by a few years, on the other hand, had unfortunately been moving further and further away from the good life she had lived so beautifully during my childhood and youth. Multiple major surgeries and the devastation of pharmaceuticals robbed her of the ability to make her own choices or experience the goodness of her life. Her death was slow and painfully heart-wrenching, not only for her but for those who had known her earlier. The death she died was brought on by diseases which ravished her and took away the very essence of who she had been. Hers was not a beautiful or a good death. There was such a pronounced difference in the two ways of ending the journey. But each was consistent with the way life moved toward that inevitable event which no one could experience for them.

A dimension to truth in dying and death has gotten more airing in the last half-century. It is the question of an attending physician speaking truthfully to his patient. There are still physicians who believe the terminally ill patient should not be told of the seriousness of her illness lest she lose hope, resign herself to helplessness and surrender her will-to-live. Some doctors believe their role as healers demands the confident assertion that all is being done to restore the patient to good health. Cure, not care, is their mandate. For some of them this is a sensitive and personal matter. To acknowledge that as far as they are able to tell the patient has reached a terminal phase is an assault on their healing powers. They have not yet come to grips with their own mortality and sometimes see themselves as the essential means of healing rather than an instrument of care and healing. Usually the relationship of that kind of physician and his or her patient is one of clinical sterility rather than human and humane cooperation.

John Hinton has this to say about the doctor's role:

> The doctor's ability to cure and bring relief usually sustains him in his work—and in his own self-esteem. He can feel very threatened at having to admit failure to a person who is depending on him. He may dread having to admit outright to his patient, whom he may know very well, that he is not going to survive….Acting as if the patient were not mortally ill does, in many ways, make it easier for the doctor to maintain his usual professional front. He need not question too deeply the ethics of his deceit if this deception is one that his patient wants and finds comforting….The authority and dignity of the doctor remains intact and the patient relies on him. An authority that needs buttressing by the assumption of impossible therapeutic powers is inherently imperfect, however, and certainly a doctor does not need to claim omnipotence to retain his patient's confidence. Perhaps a doctor's pretense to healing powers that he does not possess is culpable but it is usually less hurtful than a retreat from failure into cynicism, apparent indifference or the actual avoidance of dying patients. (37–38)

Sometimes it is not the physician who provides the opportunity for truth in death and dying. It may be another medical attendant, a hospital chaplain, or perhaps a close friend or family member who establishes such a rapport with the patient that the truth may be spoken in love. The integrity of the relationship allows the patient to explore the questions of his life and death supported by the mediating listening and caring of the compassionate other. This can symbolize the powerful role of truth in human relationships and work with the patient in grappling with the meaningfulness of his human life and arriving at a meaningful interpretation of his death. Obviously, a person who has not come to grips with his own death as a meaningful event can offer little support at such a time. But the person who can accept the meaningfulness of human death faces such a situation with two basic resources—the religious tradition or heritage or the underpinning of her life's basic beliefs and her own authentic humanity in which the divine depth has its indefinably essential place. Since each human life should have its own dignity, it is appropriate that each life have some recognition of its value. That is the basic purpose of a funeral or memorial service for the religious person or, if life has been lived from another perspective, at least a gathering of family and friends to share and remember the deceased person's life. In some appropriate form loved ones should gather to celebrate who he was and to recognize the loss brought on by his death. It need not be a large gathering or a solemn one. Think of the various funeral rites around the world including the famed New Orleans jazz processionals or Irish wakes. How sad when it all ends with the mortician taking the body away much as the garbage man collects waste materials from one's household. That is why I said earlier I have a hard time getting used to the practice of there being no formal or public acknowledgement of a person's life.

One of the most meaningful ceremonies I was involved in had only three of us there for the burial—the close friend who had asked if I would officiate, the mortician, and I. The old retired man had no living relatives and had lived a reclusive life with no other known friends than the loving person who would not let him leave this life without acknowledging that his life had its own dignity. I contrast that with a memorial service I attended for a retired person who had lots of friends. His family, and friends, some of whom had come from quite a distance away, went on for over an hour with one funny story after another of a side of him of which not everyone was aware. In it all there was love, respect, dignity and incredible appreciation for who he was and what he had done with his life as it touched so many persons so deeply. Arnold Toynbee speaks to the importance of closure in a funeral rite:

> But however diverse man's funerary rites have been they have all had a common signification. They have signified that a human being has a dignity in virtue of his being human; that his dignity survives his death; and that therefore his dead body must not simply be treated as garbage and be thrown away like the carcass of a dead non-human creature, or like a human being's worn-out boots or clothes. (59)

Sharing in coping with death

Even if a person is able to establish a true relationship with the dying, it does not necessarily follow that an appropriate mode of assisting in a good death has been found. A person is always involved not only with the dying person but with others. Each situation has its variations on the theme. These variations are affected by a complex of factors including the attitude of the family and the wishes of the dying person and her family regarding funeral rites or memorial services. It is far different to share with a person whose spouse has been deeply loved and whose final separation is an irreparable loss than with one whose marriage ceased to exist in any but a formal and legal manner before the onset of dying. Now, the death of the spouse is seen not as a loss but as the answer to a tangled problem which found no prior solution.

Sharing with the family may be no more, nor less, than a single courtesy visit following notification of death leaving them free to share intimately with those they choose. It may also be the sustained sharing which continues through preparations for and conducting the funeral or memorial service. It also may be continued sharing in their grief-work for months after the death. It is not the length of time spent with them but the depth of the relationship which counts. Again Elisabeth Kubler-Ross is insightful, "It is not the length of work you spend with the patient but how deeply you dare to be involved and really share. This is what makes counseling and helping dying patients so gratifying." (85) For decades readers and listeners have found her five stages of dying helpful: 1) denial, 2) rage and anger, 3) bargaining, 4) resignation or defeat, and 5) acceptance or victory. She acknowledges the fluidity of the paradigm but finds it useful for understanding stages of death's incursion into life. This pattern may occur in sequence for some people while for others one or more of the stages may be of short duration. The stages are also useful for dealing with other separations like a child going off to college, divorce, extended military deployments, loss of a long-time job or position, or divorce.

Usually, many persons are involved with the dying person, sharing the final journey toward death. For some families the journey precipitates real or projected guilt at not having found as meaningful a life with the dying person as they now believe they could have. In this ambivalent situation they may feel guilty for not having achieved a genuine human relationship with the patient. While there is no universal answer to this ambivalence, a person sensitive to the lives of those involved, particularly the humanity of the dying, is in a better position to offer what she is primarily capable of—a supportive presence expressing the divine depth of the human experience poignantly felt at its boundaries. The caring person cannot take from the family the emptiness and loss of final separation. She can stand with them in the loss as one who affirms the value of life and the meaningfulness of death. This support is so important even though she may be no more able than others to explain rationally why death should have cut off this particular person's life at this particular time.

It is important to point to the importance of "grief work" at this juncture. Every death needs closure. Grief work is the process of bringing that about. We vary greatly in what constitutes grief work for each of us. It is not a matter of how long one grieves, though religions have ritualized the process and prescribe specific periods of time and definite rituals and acts to be observed.

Support groups are vital for persons suffering from acute grief. This is one of the many essential services hospices provide. In these groups a person heals as she shares her grief with trust in the honesty and integrity of persons who feel her pain, loss, and loneliness. Erich Lindemann offers help in understanding acute grief:

> The picture shown by persons in acute grief is remarkably uniform. Common to all is the following syndrome: sensations of somatic distress occurring in waves lasting from twenty minutes to an hour at a time, a feeling of tightness in the throat, choking with shortness of breath, need for sighing, and an empty feeling in the abdomen, lack of muscular power, and an intense subjective distress as tension or mental pain. The patient soon learns that these waves of discomfort can be precipitated by visits, by mentioning the deceased, and by receiving sympathy. There is a tendency to avoid the syndrome at any cost, to refuse visits lest they should precipitate the reaction, and to keep deliberately from thought all references to the deceased. (187–188)

Most persons following the death of one who has been intimately close to them will not experience so severe a process. Lindemann's more general five points in grief have wider application: 1) somatic distress, 2) preoccupation with the image of the deceased, 3) guilt, 4) hostile reactions, and 5) loss of patterns of conduct. Lindemann observes that for some persons there may be a sixth element 6) appearance of traits of the deceased in the behavior of the bereaved. (189) He goes on to note factors affecting the duration of the grief experience:

> The duration of a grief reaction seems to depend upon the success with which a person does *the grief work,* namely emancipation from the bondage to the deceased, readjustment of the environment in which the deceased is missing, and the formation of new relationships. (189)

The most accessible work on grief is the little book, *Good Grief,* by Granger Westberg,[2] which has been of immense help to thousands over several decades.

Special cases abound standing outside normal shared experiences in terminal illness. For example, the case of a child who dies as a result of abuse by his parents, the aged person who outlives the compassionate care of any who feel deeply bound to her, or the person whose recklessness or suicidal overtures finally led to their deliberate and intentional death. A special case brought on by advances in medical technology is that of the patient kept alive only by the bioengineering of the modern hospital. It is a different matter to share in the emotionally charged situation between life and death with the father and mother who decide to direct that heroic measures cease, opting for death for their vegetating son, than with the family who demands that death be forestalled no matter how long the process or how high the cost.

In this labyrinthine morass nothing less than maturity, learned experiences, and a strong ethical sense will suffice. No book, video, or workshop can provide urgently desired answers. The best that can be provided is an awareness of the intricacy of the human situation and the universal need of men and women to have someone at hand in facing their own death whose life is relatively free of illusory fleeing from death—someone who has integrated it into their own convictions of life *coram Deo*—under or before God.

[1] For fuller elaboration of her treatment of death and dying, especially her well-known model of moving from denial to acceptance, see her *On Death and Dying* (1969) and *Questions and Answers on Death and Dying* (1972).

[2] Granger Westberg, *Good Grief* (1962). Westberg has done the nearly impossible. He has expressed the insights we have noted in others and put them into an easily grasped context of our own loss and the need to work through it. The frequently used imprecation, "Good Grief!" which Charles Schultz brought to the forefront in his comic strip "Peanuts" is, by Westberg, turned into the very avenue by which a person comes back from a loved one's end of the journey to resume a positive, healthy life. For more on Schultz's delving into the serious questions of life see Robert L. Short, *Gospel According to Peanuts* (1964).

Chapter 7

Coping through hospice—
a better way of living and dying

One of the most amazing and effective means of coping with death has come about in the past half century or so. The hospice movement was begun by Dame Cicely Saunders, a physician who founded St. Christopher's Hospital in a residential suburb of London in 1967.[1] How appropriate that her own death came in that same Hospice in 2005 at the age of 87. She was convinced that terminally ill patients could be treated more humanely and compassionately than they were being cared for in the dehumanized and overly institutionalized approach in hospitals. She urged doctors and nurses to refocus their intentions from curing the patient to caring for the patient.[2] She brought her enthusiastic and sound approach to Yale Medical School and Hospital in 1963. In a little over a decade the first hospice in the United States, the Connecticut House in New Haven, came into being in 1974. Soon there were several hospices being formed throughout the United States.

It is my privilege to have been deeply involved for almost two decades with the Hospice of Kitsap County, Washington, a stand-alone hospice founded in 1979 by a group of dedicated physicians and other volunteers. These remarkable people shared Dame Saunder's vision and commitment and worked tirelessly to establish hospice as a viable option for persons with terminal illness and with their families. I have served as a respite care volunteer, the president of the Board of Trustees, and in many other volunteer positions and am convinced hospice is the most incredible organization in which I have ever been involved including the academic world, the church, social service organizations, and the military. It transcends differences of race, ethnicity, social class, religion, politics and all other divisions that separate people from one another. It truly provides a better way of living and dying.

There are many types of hospices including non-profit and profit based ones. There are those that have an avowed religious connection and those that are part of a hospital or clinic. Whatever the type, there is in each of them a profound spiritual commitment to caring for the terminally ill and their loved ones with the highest level of professional and personal care. The staff of Hospice of Kitsap County, including over 100 well-trained volunteers, works together as a unified team whose primary focus is the well-being of the patient and his or her family. More can be learned about this remarkable agency by visiting its website at www.hospicekc.org. Several other websites provide valuable information on hospice.[3]

In 2008 Hospice of Kitsap County opened a hospice care center providing a state-of-the-art facility not only for patients but for their loved ones to be with them as much as they like in this last stage of life's journey. Hospice has been praised without exception from persons in the community who have had hospice care. This praise has not been confined to those who have had the services of Hospice of Kitsap County but has been the case also with everyone else with whom I have talked regardless of the geographic location of the hospice throughout the United States.

Often when I mentioned my involvement with hospice someone would say something like, "My Mother was under hospice care in another state and we don't know how we would have been able to make that final journey without that absolutely incredible care." That was the case with my sister when her husband became a hospice patient.

My sister and her husband continued to live in the southern city where she and I were born and grew up. They met when they were in college and had over fifty years of married life together. He was a kind, gentle, courteous man who loved his family, his church, and his community. After his retirement he enjoyed golfing weekly with his foursome at a local public course. He enjoyed even more helping others through tireless service to his church. Over the past few years his health deteriorated and my sister was once again marvelously taking on the care-taker role she had performed so well with our Mother's long illnesses. In the last week of his life she took him to the hospital where the attending physician recommended he go under hospice care. She took him home and hospice workers were there immediately beginning the work which they do so magnificently. Their son and daughter and their families came from some distance and stayed beside him. Hospice care-givers were more attentive than anyone had anticipated, devoting more time, attention, and professionally compassionate care than could have been expected. He died without pain with his family gathered around him to say their last goodbyes. What a blessing hospice was even for those few days. As so many others have said, "We only wish he had had that unbelievable care sooner."

These all too brief relationships are harder on everyone than more extended ones. A longer involvement means deeper relationships and greater opportunity for bonding and helping the patient and his family to meet their needs in this final phase of the journey. To be given the opportunity to become a respite care giver and to be notified even before the first visit is made that he has died is difficult. Even more difficult is to make only one or two visits and have that mysterious bond between volunteer and patient occur with promise of so much more then to get word that he has died. Like the rest of the mourners the memorial service becomes an important means of healing for the volunteer as for others close to the patient.

Hospice has an enviable reputation and receives broad community-wide support. For example, one of the local Rotary Clubs has been involved continuously with hospice since 1982. Several of the Rotary Club's members have served as president of the Board and in other capacities of leadership. The Club contributed over $100,000 toward the construction of a resident care center and has been involved in a hands-on way with landscaping and maintaining the grounds.

When hospice was not widely known there were many questions which reflected lack of knowledge or understanding rather than objections. Some physicians and other medical personnel assumed that if they made a prognosis of six months or less of life expectancy they would be encouraging the patient to give up and lose his will to live. Others felt that such acknowledgement would be an admission of defeat on their part since the only objective they would accept was a cure. Others felt that there is always the possibility that some medical breakthrough would come about and the patient would not be able to avail herself of that cure.

Occasionally a person will remark, "Isn't working with the terminally ill terribly depressing?" Quite the contrary! Persons who voluntarily commit themselves to a hospice approach have come to terms with their death. I have yet to find a single one of them morbid or depressed. While they vary, as do the rest of society, in the extent of support desired they are invariably persons of integrity who have come to terms with life and death and are ready to make the final part of their life's journey. No one becomes a hospice patient without the recommendation of his or her physician and the willingness of their family in addition to their own desire to become involved in hospice care.

The hospice movement received a quantum boost when the well-known comedian and columnist Art Buchwald became a hospice patient. He spoke to numerous organizations and published an entertaining and enlightening book, *Too Soon to Say Goodbye*, in which he recounts the exceptional care he received as a hospice patient in Washington, D.C. Many well-known celebrities visited him regularly and spread the word about the virtues and values of hospice. One of the finest tributes to him was the song his dear friend Carly Simon wrote using the title of his book.

Hospice uses a holistic approach in which an Interdisciplinary Group (IDG) meets regularly to assure that the patient and his or her loved ones are receiving appropriate care and treatment. A patient is free at any time to leave the program without prejudice against possible later return. All hospices have administrative directors as well as necessary medical and support personnel. The staff includes specially trained nurses and medical assistants who are on call round the clock. Most hospice care is provided in the patient's home, but there are also patients in nursing homes or assisted living facilities as well as resident care centers where these are available. In addition to the medical staff there are home health aides providing hygienic care for the patient on a regular basis. There are also trained social workers and spiritual counselors, usually called chaplains, who work as vital members of the Interdisciplinary Group (IDG). A staff of administrative personnel, some of whom are volunteers, rounds out the agency's human resources. A director of volunteers recruits, trains, and supervises all volunteers, including respite care givers, assuring that continuing education is provided for them and they are kept current on applicable procedures and rules and regulations affecting them.

Hospice of Kitsap County[4] as I mentioned earlier, is a stand-alone Hospice whose financial base is the revenues received from Medicare and Medicaid, Tricare, and other insurance programs. It also relies on annual apportionments from the United Way of Kitsap County, contributions from organizations and individuals including memorial gifts, and receipts from fund raising events such as Whale of a Run, which has been sponsored for several years by the Doctors' Clinic. None of this would be possible if the community as a whole were not convinced that hospice exceeds everyone's expectations in providing the best possible way of facing death while living life. It is life affirming, not death denying.

A number of books have been written by persons involved in the hospice movement which confirm why hospice is a special kind of coping. Among the best of these is *Dying Well* by Ira Byock, a physician who has served as president of the American Academy of Hospice and Palliative Medicine. His book starts with a moving account of his father's death and continues with the real-life experiences of patients he has known and cared for in hospice. You will no doubt find those personal experiences encouraging and inspiring. Once you have visited the website www.dyingwell.org you will probably find yourself returning and recommending it to others. Two practical, warm, honest and oft times humorous books by hospice nurses are also of great help. Maggie Callanan and Patricia Kelley wrote *Final*

Gifts: Understanding the Special Awareness, Needs and Communications of the Dying which was published in 1997. In 2009 Maggie Callanan provided *Final Journeys: A Practical Guide for Bringing Care and Comfort at the End of Life* in a paperback edition.

Hospice is more than a social service agency. It is a living expression of love and care which only comes to life in the stories of the people who are part of it. In reading the extraordinary stories which follow I think you will be able to grasp the meaning, depth, and power of hospice care.

I came to know Mary Elizabeth Duchaine (Mary Beth) when I was serving my first term on the Board and she was Director of Clinical Services. In time, when the Executive Director moved out of state, the Board selected her to assume that leadership role. It was my pleasure to introduce her to Rotary where with her bubbly personality she enhanced the long standing ties the Rotary Club had with hospice. We shared good times and hard times. Personal bonds between staff and board and the community were strengthened. Even though as an organization we struggled financially she was ever optimistic and hopeful that we would be able to increase the support needed to assure hospice not only survived but expanded its vital services to the community. Under her leadership ties with the local medical community were also richly enhanced.

We were greatly surprised and saddened when she shared with us that she had been diagnosed with terminal cancer.[5] It was characteristic of her that she stayed on in her position as long as she could, giving all the energy and strength she could muster to a very demanding job. In return, she received abundantly the love of all those with whom she worked. My personal bonds with her and her husband Richard had been widened when I performed the wedding ceremony for their daughter in their lovely home in its sylvan setting overlooking the bay. As the weeks advanced she became the recipient of the services she had been so lovingly providing. I was honored and inspired by every visit with her at home. She reaffirmed for me what I had long seen as one of the most astounding features of hospice—a person on the last stage of life's journey willingly letting someone else into her life. There is such a depth and beauty in that openness that the giver of services becomes the receiver of life, joy, and peace.

On the night of her passing from this life to the next her devoted husband Richard, a nurse whom she knew well, and a volunteer with a special musical talent made that transition as peaceful and beautiful as one could imagine. A day or so earlier she had guided us in planning her memorial celebration. The local Roman Catholic Church allowed the service to be held in its beautiful building since her own Episcopal Church building was far too small for the anticipated number who would mourn her death as we celebrated her life. Richard, played the organ magnificently. Several of her friends formed a choir for the occasion and sang angelically. A large and diverse congregation of grateful people thanked God for His gift to us of her life and devotion to hospice.[6] It was evident to us all that hospice is truly a better way of living and dying.

As Paul Harvey would have said, "and now for the rest of the story." Hospice of Kitsap County was fortunate to have as Mary Beth's successor a retired Navy Captain, Jim Pledger, whose naval specialty was finance. He had received a Masters Degree in Finance from the Naval Postgraduate School and after several command tours was the Comptroller of the Puget Sound Naval Shipyard when he became a member of the Hospice Board. He brought with him incredible leadership skills which took Hospice to a new level of service, support, and financial stability. Beyond that he also brought a deeply spiritual commitment to hospice as a result of his own wife's death a few years prior. He professionalized the agency without diminishing any of the humane and compassionate devotion of an expanded staff. He made it clear in all that he did that Hospice of Kitsap County was committed more than ever to the conviction that no one need die alone and that walking with the terminally ill and their loved ones in this final journey is the rarest of privileges, indeed, a sacred trust.[7]

In the past few chapters we have looked at several ways of coping with death. Even more than with intellectual exploration, we have been affected by our encounters with death and the dying. These personal experiences even more than my academic background in teaching college courses and adult workshops on death and dying since the early 1970s convince me that the most appropriate means of coping with death in contemporary society involves the resources of hospice where this is possible. If we are fortunate we die a death appropriate to the life we have lived. Hospice gives us the opportunity to make that a reality.

My personal experiences with several people who made living life their primary emphasis as they faced their own death have appeared in the previous chapters. They were vibrant, positive men and women with whom it was my privilege to walk for a while on the last part of the path of life's journey. Before I finish this book I want you to meet a few more remarkable people who graciously allowed me to become a part of their life in its final phase and whose dear ones have graciously given enthusiastic permission for their stories to be shared with you.[8]

I decided not to go back to my childhood or youth, or even to the many years of pastoral care, for stories of persons with whom I sorrowed or searched in our shared encounter with their death. Instead, I have selected some of the persons I came to know in recent years.

I still marvel that men and women imminently facing their death will let someone new into their lives and open themselves with such basic integrity and candor. Telling you their stories re-enforces my conviction that hospice is indeed in a class by itself when it comes to living life valiantly facing death. The only really important thing which we human beings have to give one another is ourselves and that must be done by both persons with complete integrity. Hospice makes that gift possible. It is a beautiful thing when that gift is given and received with graciousness and gratitude. When this happens something of incomparable worth is added to the lives of both the giver and the receiver and often to the lives of those around them. In the best sense of the word it is a sacred blessing.

Perhaps meeting these remarkable men and women even if you cannot know their names or other identifying information about them will awaken in you recognition of someone whom you have known and from whom you have learned about death and life. They were real people like you and me who laughed and loved, cared and cried, hoped and helped and then had to set it all aside to say one last time, "Goodbye my dear I have to go now."

Hopefully introducing these men and women to you will enrich your life. Knowing each one of them has certainly made my life immeasurably better.

Let me introduce you to Pat, "a very classy lady". She was the Volunteer Coordinator for hospice when I retired from the Navy Chaplaincy and applied for the open position of Spiritual Counselor/Chaplain. I was interviewed but did not get the position. I wanted to be involved with hospice anyway so I enrolled for volunteer training. Pat conducted the forty hours of training admirably. It was an amazing opportunity for friendship for both of us as we talked about the new venture I was embarking on as a hospice volunteer. I learned so much from her and my classmates. For example, I was used to using the euphemistic first person plural from my professorial days. We were engaged in an exercise teaching us how to work with patients helping them get from their hospital bed to the bathroom and back. I said to my partner a middle-aged woman, as we returned to the hospital bed, "would we like to get in bed now?" She curtly replied, "I would but we would not." The class howled and I learned a valuable lesson.

Pat gave me a bit of advice at the end of the week's training: "For God's sake don't wear a coat and tie when you go to see your patients." I also had a stipulation for her. She was not to let my patients know anything about my background. I wanted to go simply as one human-being to another human-being without any of the baggage of position or status. Pat honored that request throughout our relationship and it proved to be the right thing to do.

Pat served hospice well for a number of years, then decided to retire long before we anticipated she would. She had been retired only a few weeks when she and her husband came back from their first adventure very much aware that something was not right. After careful medical diagnosis, it was determined that she had only a short while to live.

I was privileged to conduct her memorial service at a lovely place hospice had used for some of its celebratory events. Her husband, daughter and son, and other family members, beloved former colleagues, and numerous other friends remembered her for her forthright and unassailable candor as they thanked God for her. She had given so much to hospice and now received so much from it.

This next encounter may sound familiar to you since you were introduced to this special couple in Chapter 2 (pages 36–37). I believe their story is worth sharing in this context of hospice care. Hospice offered her the services of a volunteer respite care giver but she declined feeling that she should be able to take care of her husband by herself all the time with the assistance of hospice nurses and home health aides. The social worker persuaded her to at least let a volunteer come by and get acquainted; she could then make up her mind. She agreed and I went at the appointed time. We had a pleasant visit and an appointment for the following week was arranged. The first few times I went I sat on a stool beside her husband who by that time had lost his ability to speak. What a marvelous nonverbal conversation always ensued. He would squeeze my hand and look so expressively with his eyes as we talked about things that interested him. Her confidence grew and she began to run short errands while I sat with him. In time he could go no further. She called me early one Saturday morning telling me he had died about midnight and that she had changed his pajamas and the bed linens, bathed him and shaved him and sat beside him until the morning came and she called the funeral director. In an age when many people run from death here was a sturdy, valiant person who met it head on and made life not death the conqueror. She became an incredible hero to me and I have had the joy of her friendship for almost two decades.

Earlier in the book I expressed the idea that a good death would be one which was appropriate to a person's life. I mentioned that in reference to my own father's death. Now I want to share with you an encounter with a man who was fortunate enough to have a death appropriate to his life. I had known this couple long before he became a hospice patient. They had moved here from another state where she, an ordained minister, had been a hospice chaplain. When he went under hospice care they requested me as their volunteer. I was honored to do so. I stopped by once or twice a week and we enjoyed open and honest dialogue about life and death. Time came when a hospital bed was put in their living room. One day I stopped by after teaching my college class and greeted him though he seemed unable to respond. His wife and I sat talking quietly. She had playing softly in the background a CD of hymns. We both heard him gasp and got up and went to either side of his bed. I held his hand; she wiped his face with a cool cloth. When the words of the familiar hymn were sung—"when I close my eyes in death"—he breathed his last and was no longer with us. That was mystical and dramatic; it was also an appropriate death for the life he had lived. Fortunate indeed!

Sometimes a loved one will call the volunteer and say, "My husband has just passed, what do I do now?" When that happens I have been able to tell her with confidence to call hospice and they would be there immediately and guide her through this devastating experience. That is one of the many ways hospice meets peoples' needs. I know of this first hand. A close friend of mine called me in the middle of the night telling me his beloved wife whom I had seen only a few short hours earlier had died. By the time I got to their home in twenty minutes or so the hospice nurse whom he had called just before he called me was like a ministering angel getting everything in order in the passage from life to death. They were a beautiful couple whose friendship I treasured long before her becoming a hospice patient. He and I worked closely on the adult education program of our church and she sang in the choir. Sometimes she sang a solo accompanying her-self on the autoharp. It was always an inspiring and thrilling experience to hear her sweet angelic voice. She was deeply mourned and greatly missed. Hospice was there with that special kind of caring.

There is now another wonderful man whom I want you to meet. He was being attentively cared for by his daughter and her husband with whom he lived. They were devoutly religious and asked if I could visit him on Sundays so that they could go to church. It worked out fine for all of us. He had retired from the Navy as a Master Chief Petty Officer. We bonded quickly and told sea stories to one another. We had been at many of the same places though not at the same time. As he slipped further away he would not let go of the ranks we both had held in our active duty years. He always referred to me as Commander and saluted when he had the strength to do so. I tried to get past this but couldn't. When I visited him for what was to be the last time he saluted me and said, "Commander, I respectfully request permission to leave my post." I returned his salute and replied, "Permission granted Master Chief." He left his post and moved on to his new duty station not long after.

That reminds me of another Navy veteran and his wife whom I wish you could have known. They had become deeply involved in a local church which meant a great deal to them. Life was better than it had ever been. His memorial service at the church was well attended expressing how deeply they had become a part of that supportive community. Each time I approached his front door I had to ring the ship's bell he had mounted there and call out, "Request permission to come aboard," From inside he would reply, "Permission granted." They were a loving couple who obviously were grateful they had found each other. She brightened up each time he spoke to her and he was at peace when she was near. She called me early one morning to tell me he had passed away. She told me her sister had flown out from the Midwest and was with her. After her sister arrived she stood by her husband's bed-side and told him he need not worry about her since her sister was there to help take care of her. He smiled though he was unable to speak. She continued, "I love you and am giving you permission to go to heaven; I will be alright." It was not long before he quietly made that peaceful transition from this life to the next. There are many patients who are not able to let go and move from this life to the next until they hear from their loved one that they will be able to make it without them. They appear to need permission from the one they love before they can make that last step of the final journey.

For a year after the hospice resident care center opened I visited patients there once a week. Those were very short relationships. Nevertheless, many of them were very meaningful. There were many men and women who enriched my life by letting me become part of their deeply personal encounter with death. I cannot say enough in praise of the dedicated staff that cares so compassionately for all patients and their families.

I am only going to share the stories of two men who were there about the same time. Both of them had families who loved them and were with them often. The first man was a retired professional musician. His room was a sanctuary for me each Sunday when I visited. He had lovely music—sometimes classical, sometimes smooth jazz or well chosen standards -- playing each time I went in. We talked of music, literature, and the arts, of beauty, and wonder, and things that had meant much to both of us. We talked of family and friends and the privilege of sharing the joys and sorrows of life with persons who mattered. There was that inexplicable bond which occurs more often than we have a right to expect. I did not learn of another side of him—the practical iconoclastic joker—until his delightful memorial service at the church where he had grown up. How privileged I felt to have gotten to know him even if for so short a time. His daughter expressed appreciation for my visits and remarked, "You know if Dad had known you were a retired Navy Chaplain, he would never have let you into his life as he did." How exhilarating to be just one human being accepted by another human being opening our very souls to one another!

The other man was quite different but just as special in his own way. He had worked outdoors most of his life and after the death of his wife and his retirement he had moved here to be near his beloved sister. I happened to know and admire her through Rotary. He and I had such easy, enjoyable conversations. He was warm and outgoing and dearly loved by all the staff. When I went to see him he was usually sitting up in a chair dressed in a cowboy shirt and jeans. The last time I saw him he said, "Well, I've come to the end of the trail and it's time for me to ride on over the horizon." He made that last ride only a few days later.

There is just one more person whom I want you to meet. Then I will reluctantly stop sharing these experiences. I got to know him through Rotary rather than hospice. We worked together on many projects. He was always quiet and unassuming. I knew he had retired as a senior executive of a major global corporation. After his retirement he and his lovely wife had chosen to move here to be near their family.

I remember with pleasure working beside him on a children's playground he had been instrumental in getting underway. I deeply treasure days we rang the bell for the Salvation Army at Christmas time as our Rotary engaged in this contribution to the community. It was only at his memorial service that I learned more of the man whom I had not known. He had been a driving force in his company and was respected far beyond our small circle of friends as evidenced by the men and women who had flown in from great distances to celebrate his life and pay tribute to him.

After his retirement he and his wife had gone overseas to serve as an advisor/consultant for a U.S. agency helping European businesses learn more about American business practices. After a ski trip they returned to the country where they were living and working. He was not feeling well and was treated by a local doctor. Some months after returning to the United States he developed medical problems which became more severe. He was in and out of both our local hospital and the near-by major medical center more times than I can recount.

Never once had I, or anyone else at the memorial service, heard him complain. Through the painful ordeal of his suffering he kept telling us all how good life had been and how much he appreciated who he was and what he had—his beautiful wife and life-long companion and friend, their fine children and grandchildren, his friends, and the respect of the community. If ever a person had justification for railing against what had happened to him through no fault of his own, he did. Yet he chose not to. He left us an inexpressible gift by living his life as fully as possible knowing everyday he was facing death and that could not be forestalled. As he had done so successfully in college and in his illustrious career, he was committed to making the very most of what he had. He lived and died in such a way that any one who knew his story would be convinced that he had truly found a better way of living and dying.

These are but a few of the remarkable men and women I have had the privilege of knowing and wish you could have known too. There is no doubt but that my life is better for their having let me into their lives and teaching me so much about death and life. One of the things most of us want to do as life shortens is to tell our story to someone who cares. That is an area where hospice makes a tremendous difference. Maybe these stories families have shared with you have opened possibilities for you to remember how your own life has been enriched by some of the extraordinary persons you have met along life's journey. Maybe reflecting on these encounters has encouraged you to get to know others along the way who have so much to share about life and death. At least I hope so.

[1] See Shirley Du Boulay and Marianne Rankin, *Cicely Saunders: The Founder of the Modern Hospice Movement* (2007).

[2] For a comprehensive treatment of this important concept see David Clark, *Cicely Saunders—Founder of the Hospice Movement: Selected Letters, 1959–1999* (2005) and also, Cicely Saunders and David Clark, *Cicely Saunders: Selected Writings,* 1958–2004 (2006).

[3] See www.aahpm.org (American Academy of Hospice and Palliative Medicine); www.americanhospice.org (information on grieving, workshops, links, etc.); www.hospicecare.com (International Association for Hospice and Palliative Care—IAHPC); www.hospicefoundation.org (defines hospice care); www.nhpco.org (largest non-profit membership organization representing hospice and palliative care programs and professionals in the United States).

[4] Information about Hospice of Kitsap County may be obtained by visiting www.hospicekc.org and by consulting their Annual Reports, *Sojourner,* and *Newsline* as well as numerous articles which have appeared over the years in the Kitsap Sun, the local newspaper.

[5] Hospice of Kitsap County *Sojourner,* Winter 2001, "A Fond Farewell" and *Hospice of Kitsap County: Annual Report 2002: Dedicated in Loving Memory Patricia Wicks 1938–2003 & Mary Elizabeth Duchaine 1940–2003.*

[6] *The Seattle Times,* obituary for Mary Elizabeth Duchaine, March 31, 2003.

[7] Hospice of Kitsap County *Newsline,* January–March 2002.

[8] These stories are shared with the gracious permission of persons most intimately involved with the person encountered. In most cases their names have been omitted to protect their privacy. It was amazing how each personal representative who signed permission agreements and authorization for healthcare information release expressed their appreciation for having their loved ones story shared with others.

Conclusion

A conclusion is supposed to be an end, or at least an ending. It implies that all that was considered important to the problem or issue has been written, at least for now. This seems inappropriate to the mystery of death. Perhaps Søren Kierkegaard was right after all: "...as death is the last of all, so shall this be the last thing we say about it: it is inexplicable." (112) Yet, every experience we have with death is bound to affect the way we perceive the mystery and shape our coping with it. While we cannot definitively resolve the mystery there are some things we can say about death. I have tried to do that.

Many intriguing roads have not been taken. There is something holy about death in the sense that Rudolf Otto treats the Holy. As he develops the term, we are attracted, fascinated, and curious about it while at the same time we are repelled, disturbed, and confounded by it. Like moths to the light we are drawn by its glare even while we want to flee from it. At least some of the time it illuminates the sacredness of human life.

The first workshop on death and dying I held was for a group of adults at Eureka College, Illinois, in the summer of 1963. We started with the participants acting out Tolstoy's marvelous treatment in *The Death of Ivan Ilyich*. In response to the question I asked early on: "What are your expectations for the workshop?" I received the answer: "I don't know exactly, but the first session was warm and friendly and it felt comfortable to be hearing death talked about because it is a subject that is difficult and embarrassing to talk about with family and friends." In facing death with integrity we recover some of the warmth, tenderness, and comfort we share with one another simply because we are human. In experiences of profound silence we know our humanity at its deepest and are opened to its divine origin and destiny.

The most frequently asked question at the beginning of the college courses on death and dying I have taught was, "What do you say to someone who is dying or to the loved one of someone who has died?" My response was more akin to Job than to his well-meaning friends—silence is more eloquent than words. A simple, "I'm sorry," spoken from the heart may open doors for the mind. Even if it doesn't, it conveys a bond of caring. In death, as in life, the most we can do for one another is simply be there with and for each other. The type and quality of the relationship directs the conversation and its content. Who you are is more crucial than what you say. The playwright is once again insightful: "Don't talk at all!—show me."[1]

I hope this book has shown some ways of facing death which make living life all the richer. It has probably left more questions unanswered than either of us would have liked. If that is the case I hope you will seek better answers than you have found here and share them with others who, like you, want to live life at its fullest and die a good, appropriate death.

There really can be no conclusion to facing death; only a place to stop with the hope of continuing again.

[1] This line is from Alan Jay Lerner and Frederick Loewe, *My Fair Lady* (1964).

Epilogue

I will die. I do not know when, or where, or how. Perhaps I will die a quick death like my father who died at 69. The marvel of a bypass surgery has contributed to my already having passed that by over ten years. Or, maybe I will die a prolonged, agonizing, transforming death like my mother. She was 65. Or, it could be that I would be in the wrong place at the wrong time and die of an accident brought on by a drunk or drugged driver. It could even be that I will simply go to sleep one evening and not wake up the next morning. Who knows? The only thing certain is that it will happen. All the other questions are open-ended. I cannot do much about that. What I can do something about is make the best preparations to assist my wife, Blossom, and my daughter, Amelia, as my personal representatives—that is the current term for what used to be called executrixes. They will have the burden of settling my unfinished business and sharing what might be left with my family and the organizations or agencies I especially want to benefit from what I am able to pass on to them. They will also be responsible for arranging for appropriate celebration of my life as they at the same time mourn my death.

As I finish this book, I want to share with you how I have gone about trying to assist them. I shall not impose on you the details. I simply want to say this is the way I have gone about it and hope you too will anticipate your death so that the ending can be as consistent as possible with your life's journey.

Once a quarter, I update my guidance to them with current figures for accounts, pertinent addresses and phone numbers, and my thoughts at the time as to how I would like to be remembered. The material contains 1) step-by-step instructions with financial statements, an obituary for the local newspaper, and notes on the memorial service, 2) a brochure on People's Memorial Service for handling the disposal of my body by means of cremation, 3) a brochure "What to do when a death occurs", 3) certified copies of DD214—discharge papers from the Navy, and 4) my birth certificate.

The Step-by-step instructions have contact information for 1) persons to be notified, 2) agencies such as Social Security Administration and Defense Finance and Accounting Service, 3) my lawyer, accountant, and broker. 4) financial institutions with account numbers, 5) insurance companies with policy numbers, and 6) universities from which I graduated and professional associations of which I am a member.

Instructions are provided for distributing assets to Hospice and other agencies I hold dear as well as to my children and their children. None of these are large amounts, but by designating them I am able to express appreciation for the ways in which they have enriched my life.

I live in the great Pacific Northwest. My children and their families live in Shanghai, China, Dothan, Alabama, St. Louis, Missouri, and Jekyll Island, Ga. I do not expect them to come to a Memorial Service for me in Bremerton. What I have requested they do is gather at a mutually agreed upon time within the first year after my death at Jekyll Island, Georgia for a memorial weekend. Each of them will have been sent a box with their share of my cremated remains. Living so far from one another they rarely get together. A final act of fatherly care is my leaving resources for them to gather with one another for a few days to live out their joys and sorrows, their remembrance of things past, as Proust would say, some of which are fondly recalled and some we wish would dissipate into the unknown and forgotten.

The memorial service in Bremerton is for my wife and friends. I will not present it in the format of the service. But,

I do want to share with you some of what I have asked to be included. I am confident the organist will choose from the rich repertoire of classical pieces for prelude and postlude. I want the congregation to sing at the beginning of the service all verses of "Now Thank We All Our God." and at the end "O Love that will not Let Me Go." In the middle I want a soloist to sing, "Of the Father's Love Begotten." Psalm 107 is to be read as a litany and I John 4:7–21 is to be the primary New Testament reading. I would like my son-in-law Terry Stansell to read the eulogy making whatever comments he chooses to make on behalf of the other children. I am asking three special friends to make brief comments. Jim Pledger, the now retired Executive Director of Hospice of Kitsap County is to comment on my involvement with Hospice. (I have often remarked that the best thing I ever did for Hospice was inviting Jim Pledger to become a member of our Board of Trustees). Steve Slaton, trusted friend and former President of our Rotary Club and one of the persons I have worked closely beside in many endeavors is to comment on my participation as a Rotarian. I will be honored for Laurie Liberty, former colleague at Chapman University and my valued friend, to comment on my life as a teacher and learner. I have asked that there not be an open microphone. Whatever anyone else has to say can be said during the reception, which is to follow immediately in the church's fellowship hall with cool jazz playing in the background. Dave Brubeck's "Take Five" never fails to move me with its sacral dimensions. When I was a high school band member I found an album of jazz by Bunk Johnson and heard his rendition of "Just a Closer Walk with Thee". I would like that played as well. This more casual experience should allow those who want to say goodbye to do so without imposed piety or attribution of saintliness which we know would violate their integrity and my own.

I hope you have found this Epilogue an encouragement to do your own thinking and planning for an appropriate recognition of both your life and your death.

Works Cited

Books and articles

Albom, Mitch. *Tuesdays with Morrie: An Old Man, a Young Man, and Life's Greatest Lessons.* New York: Broadway Books, 1997.

Athanasius. *On the Incarnation.* London: Mowbray, 1953.

Augustine. "The City of God." Tr. M. Dods. *Basic Writings of Saint Augustine.* Whitney J. Oates, ed. New York: Random House, 1948. Vol. 2, pp. 3–663.

Augustine. "The Confessions". Tr. J.G. Pilkington. *Basic Writings of Saint Augustine.* Whitney J. Oates, ed. New York: Random House, 1948. Vol. 1, pp. 3–256.

Augustine. *Writings of Saint Augustine.* Vol. 2. *On the Immortality of the Soul and Other Works. The Fathers of the Church; a New Translation.* Washington, DC: Catholic University of America Press, 1947.

Balthasar, Hans Ur von. *Origen: Spirit and Fire: a Thematic Anthology of His Writings.* Washington, DC: Catholic University of America, 2001.

Bartsch, Hans, ed. *Kerygma and Myth.* London: SPCK, 1957.

Beckett, Samuel. *Endgame.* 2nd revised ed. London: Faber and Faber, 1976.

Bellah, Robert, "Civil Religion in America." *Daedelus,* (Winter 1967). pp. 1–21.

Berdyaev, Nicholas A. *The Destiny of Man.* Tr. N. Duddington. London: Geoffrey Bles, 1937.

Berdyaev, Nicholas A. *Dream and Reality: An Essay in Autobiography.* Tr. Katherine Lampert. New York: Macmillan, 1951.

Berdyaev, Nicholas A. *The Fate of Man in the Modern World.* Tr. Donald A. Lowrie. Milwaukee: C. Morehouse, 1935.

Biggs, Charles. *The Christian Platonists of Alexandria.* Oxford: Clarendon Press, 1886.

Borkenau, Franz, "The Concept of Death," *Death and Identity.* Robert Fulton, ed. New York: John Wiley, 1965. pp. 42–56.

Bruder, Ernest, "The Distinction between Psychotherapy and Pastoral Counseling," *Medical Bulletin of the Naval Regional Medical Center and Naval Hospital.* Portsmouth, VA (Winter 1971). Vol. VI, No. 4. pp. 70–75.

Buchwald, Art. *Too Soon to say Goodbye.* New York: Random House, 2006.

Byock, Ira. *Dying Well: Peace and Possibilities at the End of Life.* New York: Riverhead Books, 1997.

Cadbury, Henry S., "Intimations of Immortality in the Thought of Jesus," *Immortality and Resurrection.* Krister Stendahl, ed. New York: Macmillan, 1965. pp. 115–149.

Callanan, Maggie. *Final Journeys: A Practical Guide for Bringing Care and Comfort at the End of Life.* Reprint ed. New York: Bantam, 2008.

Callanan, Maggie and Patricia Kelley. *Final Gifts: Understanding the Special Awareness, Needs, and Communication of the Dying.* Baltimore: Penguin, 1997.

Cannon, William R. *The Theology of John Wesley.* Nashville: Abingdon, 1946.

Cargas, Henry J. and Ann White, eds. *Death and Hope.* New York: Corpus Books, 1971.

Choron, Jacques. *Modern Man and Mortality.* New York: Macmillan, 1964. Later title, *Death and Modern Man.* New York: Macmillan, 1972.

Christ, Adolph E. "Attitudes toward Death among a Group of Acute Geriatric Psychiatric Patients," *Death and Identity.* Robert Fulton, ed. New York: John Wiley, 1965. pp. 146–152.

Clark, David. *Cicely Saunders—Founder of the Hospice Movement: Selected Letters, 1959–1999.* Oxford: Oxford University Press, 2005.

Coleman, Graham, Thpten Jinpa, and Gyurme Dorje, eds. and trans. *The Tibetan Book of the Dead.* New York: Penguin, 2007.

Connelly, Marc. *The Green Pastures: a fable suggested by Roark Bradford's southern sketches, "Ol' man Adam an' his chillun"* 38th ed. New York: Hold, Rinehart and Winston, 1967.

Corliss, Richard, Comment on death of actress Natasha Richardson in *Time Magazine,* March 30, 2009. page 22.

Cullman, Oscar, "Immortality of the Soul or Resurrection of the Dead: the witness of the New Testament," *Immortality and Resurrection.* Krister Stendahl, ed. New York: Macmillan, 1965. pp. 9-53.

Dante. *Divine Comedy: the Inferno.*

DeSpelder, Lynne Ann and Albert Lee Strickland. *The Last Dance: Encountering Death and Dying.* 9th ed. New York: McGraw-Hill, 2010.

Du Boulay, Shirley and Marianne Rankin. *Cicely Saunders: The Founder of the Modern Hospice Movement.* London: SPCK, 2007.

Feifel, Herman, ed. *The Meaning of Death.* New York: McGraw-Hill, 1965.

Ferlinghetti, Lawrence. *A Coney Island of the Mind.* New York: New Directions, 1958.

Ferre, Nels F.S. *The Christian Understanding of God.* New York: Harper, 1951.

Flew, Anthony N., "Can a Man Witness His Own Funeral?" *The Hibbert Journal,* Vol. LIV (April 1956). pp. 242-250.

Freud, Sigmund. "Thoughts for the times of War and Death". *Collected Papers.* Vol. IV. New York: Basic Books, 1959.

Fulton, Robert, ed. *Death and Identity.* New York: John Wiley, 1965.

Fulton, Robert, "The Sacred and the Secular: Attitudes of the American Public Toward Death, Funerals, and Funeral Directors." *Death and Identity.* Robert Fulton, ed. New York: John Wiley, 1965. pp. 89–105.

Fulton, Robert and Gilbert Geis, "Death and Social Values," *Death and Identity.* Robert Fulton, ed. New York: John Wiley, 1965. pp. 67–75.

Gatch, Milton. *Death: Meaning and Mortality in Christian Thought and Contemporary Culture.* Greenwich, CT: Seabury Press, 1969.

Gelpi, Donald L. *Life and Light: a Guide to the Theology of Karl Rahner.* New York: Sheed and Ward, 1966.

Glatzer, Nahum. *Franz Rosenzweig: his life and thought.* New York: Schocken, 1953.

Gorer, Geoffrey, "The Pornography of Death," *Identity and Anxiety,* Maurice Stein, Arthur J. Vidich, and David Manning White, eds. Glencoe, IL: The Free Press, 1960. pp. 402–407.

Gottlieb, Carla, "Modern Art and Death," *The Meaning of Death.* Herman Feifel, ed. New York: McGraw-Hill, 1959. pp. 157–188.

Hartshorne, Charles, "Time, Death and Eternal Life," *The Journal of Religion,* Vol. XXXII, No. 2 (April 1952), pp. 97–107.

Heidegger, Martin. *Being and Time.* Tr. John Macquarrie and Edward Robinson. London: SCM Press, 1962.

Heller, James J., "The Resurrection of Man," *Theology Today* (July 1958). pp. 217-229.

Henderson, Ian. *Myth in the New Testament.* London: SCM Press, 1952.

Hinton, John, "The Dying and the Doctor," *Man's Concern with Death.* Arnold Toynbee and others, eds. New York: McGraw-Hill, 1969. pp. 36–45.

Hoffman, Frederick J., "Mortality and Modern Literature," *The Meaning of Death.* Herman Feifel, ed. New York: McGraw-Hill, 1959. pp. 133-156.

Irion, Paul. *Funeral: Vestige or Value?* Nashville: Abingdon, 1966.

Isaacson, Walter. *Einstein: His Life and Universe.* New York: Simon & Schuster, 2007.

Jaeger, Werner, "The Greek Ideas of Immortality," *Immortality and Resurrection*. Krister Stendahl, ed. New York: Macmillan, 1965. pp.97–114.

Janson, H.W. *History of Art*. Revised ed. New York: Abrams, 1969.

Jenkins, Margie. *You Only Die Once: Preparing for the end of life with grace and gusto*. Georgetown, TX: Balcony Publishing, 2002.

The Jewish Bible: Tanakh: The Holy scriptures–the New Jewish Publication Society Translation according to the Traditional Hebrew Text: Torah* Nevi'im* Kethuvim*. New York: The Jewish Publication Society of America, 1985.

Johnson, Aubrey S. *The Vitality of the Individual in the Thought of Ancient Israel*. Cardiff: University of Wales Press, 1949.

Jung, Carl G., "The Soul and Death," *The Meaning of Death*. Herman Feifel, ed. New York: McGraw-Hill, 1959. pp.3–15.

Kavanaugh, James. *Facing Death*. Baltimore: Penguin Books, 1974.

Keck, Leander, "The Treatment of Death in the New Testament," *Perspectives on Death*. Liston Mill, ed. Nashville: Abingdon, 1970.

Kegley, Charles W. and Robert W. Bretall, eds. *The Theology of Paul Tillich*. New York: Macmillan, 1956.

Kierkegaard, Soren A., "The Decisiveness of Death," *Thoughts on Crucial Situations in Human Life: Three Discourses on Imagined Occasions*. David Swensen, ed. Milwaukie: Augsburg, 1941.

Kohler, Ludwig. *Hebrew Man*. Tr. Peter R. Ackroyd. London: SCM Press, 1956.

Kubler-Ross, Elisabeth. *Death: the Final Stage of Growth*. New York: Scribner, 1997.

Kubler-Ross, Elisabeth, "Dignity in Death," *Medical Bulletin of the Naval Regional Medical Center and Naval Hospital*. Portsmouth, Virginia. Vol. VI, No. 4 (Winter 1971). pp. 76–85.

Kubler-Ross, Elisabeth. *Questions and Answers on Death and Dying*. New York: Macmillan, 1972.

Kubler-Ross, Elisabeth and David Kessler. *On Grief and Grieving: Finding the Meaning of Grief Through the Five Stages of Loss.* New York: Scribner, 2007.

Kubler-Ross, Elisabeth. *On Death and Dying.* New York: Macmillan, 1969.

Leben angesichts des Todes: Beitrage zum theologisches Problem des Todes. Helmut Thielicke zum 60. Geburtstag. Tubingen: JCB Mohr, 1968.

Lifton, Robert J., "Psychological Effects of the Atomic Bomb on Hiroshima: The Theme of Death." *Death and Identity.* Robert Fulton, ed. New York: John Wiley, 1965. pp. 8–42.

Lindemann, Erick, "Symptomatology and Management of Acute Grief." *Death and Identity.* Robert Fulton, ed. New York: John Wiley, 1965. pp. 186-201.

Lowrie, Donald A. *Rebellious Prophet: a Life of Nicholas Berdyaev.* New York: Harper, 1960.

Luther, Martin. This quotation is in dozens of anthologies but Reference Librarians at major theological libraries have not been able to identify the exact work in which it appears.

MacLeish, Archibald. *JB.* Boston: Houghton Mifflin,1961.

Malinowski, Bronislaw. *Magic, science and religion, and other essays.* Glencoe, IL: Free Press, 1948.

Mant, A. Keith, "The Medical Definition of Death," *Man's Concern with Death.* Arnold Toynbee and others, eds. New York: McGraw-Hill, 1969. pp. 13-24.

Marcel, Gabriel. *The Mystery of Being.* Trans. Rene Hague. 2 Vols. Chicago: Henry Regnery, 1950-51.

Martin-Achard, Robert. *From Death to Life: a Study of the Development of the Doctrine of the Resurrection in the Old Testament.* London: Oliver and Boyd, 1960.

Mathews, Joseph W., "The Time My Father Died," *Motive* (January–February 1964. pp.4–9 also in Nathan Scott's *The Modern Vision of Death.* Richmond: John Knox, 1967.

May, William F., "The Conspiracy of Silence," *Christianity and Crisis,* April 16, 1962. pp. 52–56.

Mayer, Catherine, "#5 Amortality," *Time Magazine*, March 23, 2009. page 53.

Mill, Liston, ed. *Perspectives on Death.* Nashville: Abingdon, 1970.

Milton, John. *Paradise Lost.*

Mitford, Jessica. *The American Way of Death.* New York: Simon and Schuster, 1963.

Mitford, Jessica. *The American Way of Death Revisited.* New York: Vintage, 2000.

Mora, Jose Ferrater. *Being and Death.* Berkeley, CA: University of California Press, 1965.

Morgantheau, Hans, "Death in the Nuclear Age," *The Modern Vision of Death.* Nathan Scott, ed. Richmond, VA: John Knox Press, 1967. pp. 69-77.

Neale, Robert E. *The Art of Dying.* New York: Harper and Row, 1973.

The New Oxford Annotated Bible with Apocryphal/ Deuterocanonical Books. Bruce M. Metzger and Roland E. Murphy, eds. New Revised Standard Version. New York: Oxford University Press, 1991.

Nuland, Sherwin B. *How We Die: Reflections on Life's Final Chapter.* New York: Alfred A. Knopf, 1994.

Nygren, Anders. *Agape and Eros.* New and revised ed. Philadelphia: Westminster, 1953.

Otto, Rudolf. *The Idea of the Holy: An Inquiry into the Non-Rational Factor in the Idea of the Divine and its Relation to the Rational.* Tr. John W. Harvey. 2nd ed. Oxford: Oxford University Press, 1950.

Oulton, John E.L. and Henry Chadwick, eds. *Alexandrian Christianity.* Philadelphia: Westminster, 1954.

Pausch, Randy. "The Last Lecture," You Tube, December 20, 2007. *The Last Lecture.* New York: Hyperion, 2008.

Plato. *Apology, Crito, Phaedo.*

Pritchett, Rachel, "Going Green into the Ground," *Kitsap Sun* (Washington) (June 14, 2009) pp. A1, A4.

Rahner, Karl. *On the Theology of Death.* Trans. Charles H. Henkey. New York: Thomas Nelson, 1961.

Rilke, Rainer Marie. *The Notebook of Malte Laurids Brigge.* Tr. M.D. Herter. New York: Norton, 1949.

Roberts, David E. *The Grandeur and Misery of Man.* New York: Oxford University Press, 1955.

Roberts, Louis. *The Achievement of Karl Rahner.* New York: Herder and Herder, 1967.

Russell, Bertrand. *Principles of Social Reconstruction.* London: Allen and Unwin, 1916. Published in the United States under the title *Why Men Fight.* New York: Century, 1917.

Saaz, Johannes von. *Death and the Ploughman.* Tr. Ernest K. Kirmann. Chapel Hill: University of North Carolina Press, 1958.

Saunders, Cicely and David Clark. *Cicely Saunders: Selected Writings, 1958–2004.* Oxford: Oxford University Press, 2006.

Schaalman, Herman E. "Franz Rosenzweig: a voice for today," *Christian Century* (February 22, 1967). pp. 233-236.

Schultz, Charles. *Peanuts.the comic strip.*

Scott, Nathan, ed. *The Modern Vision of Death.* Richmond: John Knox Press, 1967.

Shakespeare, William. *Julius Caesar*

Shakespeare, William. *Hamlet*

Shoor, Mervyn and Mary H. Speed, "Death, Delinquency, and the Mourning Process," *Death and Identity.* Robert Fulton, ed. New York: John Wiley, 1965. pp. 201-206.

Short, Robert L. *Gospel According to Peanuts.* New York: Bantam, 1964.

Silberman, Lou H. "The Treastment of Death in the Old Testament," *Perspectives on Death.* Liston Mill, ed. Nashville: Abingdon, 1970.

Simon, Carly, "Too Soon to Say Goodbye," Art Buchwald. *Too Soon To Say Goodbye.* New York: Random House, 2006. pp. 180–181.

Smart, Ninian, "Death in the Judaeo-Christian Tradition," *Man's Concern with Death*. Arnold Toynbee and others, eds. New York: McGraw-Hill, 1969. pp. 116–121

Stendahl, Krister, ed. *Immortality and Resurrection*. New York: Macmillan, 1955.

Taylor, Jeremy. *The Rules and Exercises of Holy Living and Holy Dying*. London: J. Parker, 1866.

Tennyson, Alfred Lord. *In Memoriam.*

Thielicke, Helmut. *Christ and the Meaning of Life*. Tr. John Doberstein. New York: Harper, 1962.

Thielicke, Helmut. *Death and Life*. Trans. E.H. Schroeder. Minneapolis: Fortress Press, 1970.

Thielicke, Helmut. *A Little Exercise for Young Theologians*. Tr. Charles L. Taylor. Grand Rapids, MI: Eerdman's, 1962.

Thielicke, Helmut. *Out of the Depths*. Trans. G.W. Bromiley. Grand Rapids: Eerdman's, 1962.

Thielicke, Helmut. *The Silence of God*. Trans. G.W. Bromiley. Grand Rapids, MI: Eerdman's, 1962.

Thielicke, Helmut. *Tod und Leben: Studien zur Christlichen Anthropologie*. Tubingen: JCB Mohr, 1946.

Thielicke, Helmut. *The Waiting Father*. Trans. John Doberstein. New York: Harper, 1959.

Thomas, Dylan, "Ceremony after a Fire Raid" in *Accent Anthology: Selections from Accent, a quarterly of new literature*. Kerker Quinn and Charles Shattuck, eds. New York: Harcourt, Brace, 1971. p. 432.

Tillich, Paul. *Biblical Religion and the Search for Ultimate Reality*. Chicago: University of Chicago Press, 1955.

Tillich, Paul. *The Courage to Be*. New Haven: Yale University Press, 1952.

Tillich, Paul. "The Eternal Now," *The Meaning of Death*. Herman Feifel, ed. New York: McGraw-Hill, 1959. pp.30-38.

Tillich, Paul, "Symbols of Eternal Life," *Harvard Divinity Bulletin*. Vol. XXVI (April 1962). pp. 1-10.

Tillich, Paul. *Systematic Theology*. 3 Volumes. Chicago: University of Chicago Press, 1951-1963.

Tolstoy, Leo. *The Death of Ivan Ilyich.* New York: New American Library, 1960.

Toynbee, Arnold, "Changing Attitudes Towards Death in the Modern Western World," *Man's Concern with Death.* Arnold Toynbee and others, eds. New York: McGraw-Hill, 1968. pp. 122–132.

Toynbee, Arnold, "Death in War," *Man's Concern with Death.* Arnold Toynbee and others, eds. New York: McGraw-Hill, 1969. pp. 145–152.

Toynbee, Arnold, "Increased Longevity and the Decline of Infant Mortality." *Man's Concern with Death.* Arnold Toynbee and others, eds. New York: McGraw-Hill, 1969. pp. 153–159.

Toynbee, Arnold, "Perspectives from time, space, and nature," *Man's Concern with Death.* Arnold Toynbee and others, eds. New York: McGraw-Hill, 1969. pp. 179–184.

Toynbee, Arnold, "Traditional Attitudes Towards Death," *Man's Concern with Death.* Arnold Toynbee and others, eds. New York: McGraw-Hill, 1969. pp. 59–94.

Toynbee, Arnold and others, eds. *Man's Concern with Death.* New York: McGraw-Hill, 1969.

Troisfontaines, Roger, "Death, a Test for Love, a Condition of Freedom," *Cross Currents* (Summer 1957). pp. 201–212.

Tylor, Edward B. *Religion in Primitive Culture.* Reprint ed. Gloucester, MA: Peter Smith, 1970.

Volkert, Edmund H. and Stanley T. Michael, "Bereavement and Mental Health," *Death and Identity.* Robert Fulton, ed. New York: John Wiley, 1965. pp. 272-293.

Wahl, Charlees W., "The Fear of Death," *Death and Identity.* Robert Fulton, ed. New York: John Wiley, 1965. pp. 16–29.

Waugh, Evelyn. *The Loved One.* New York: Dell, 1954.

Weisman, Avery D. and Thomas P. Hackett, "Predilection to Death," *Death and Identity.* Robert Fulton, ed. New York: John Wiley, 1965, pp. 293-329.

Westberg, Granger. *Good Grief.* Milwaukie: Augsburg Press, 1962.

White, Hugh Vernon, "Immortality and Resurrection in Recent Theology," *Encounter* (Winter 1961), pp. 52–58.

Wilder, Amos, "Mortality and Contemporary Literature," *The Modern Vision of Death.* Nathan Scott, ed. Richmond: John Knox Press, 1967. pp. 17–44.

Williams, Colin W. *John Wesley's Theology Today.* Nashville: Abingdon, 1960.

Winston, Robert P., John Roemer, and Wallace Budge, eds. and trans. *The Egyptian Book of the Dead.* New York: Penguin, 2008.

Wolfson, Harry A., "Immortality and Resurrection in the Philosophy of the Church Fathers," *Immortality and Resurrection.* Krister Stendahl, ed. New York: Macmillan, 1965. pp. 54–96.

Yudkin, Simon, "Death and the Young," *Man's Concern with Death.* Arnold Toynbee and others, eds. New York: McGraw-Hill, 1969. pp. 46–55.

Movies, videos, and electronic media

The Bucket List. Movie 2007. DVD 2008.

Harold and Maude. Movie 1971. DVD 2000.

Love and Death, 1975. DVD 2000.

My Fair Lady, 1964. DVD 2009.

Six Feet Under, TV Series (HBO), 2001–2005. DVD 2009.

Web sites

Hospice of Kitsap County. www.hospicekc.org

The Neptune Society. www.neptunesociety.com

On Our Own Terms: Moyers on Dying.
    www.pbs.org/wnet/onourownterms.

Peoples' Memorial Association. www.peoplesmemorial.org

Additional Resources

It is problematic whether a bibliography, in addition to Works Cited, will be of value to a reader. Computer search engines, such as Google, make accessing almost anything a person wants to find relatively easy. However, I prepared my first Bibliography on Death and Dying more than forty years ago and have been adding to it ever since then. It now has more than 1500 entries. I am choosing from that work about 200 of those entries which I think would be of benefit to someone wanting to pursue certain topics further. **A work listed in Works Cited is not listed again in Additional Resources.** For convenience sake the listing is by categories.

Websites

www.abcd.caring.org (Americans for Better Care of the Dying – ABCD)

www.dyingwell.org (site created by Dr. Ira Byock author of the book by that title.)

www.endoflifecare.org (promoting excellence in end of life care. The Robert Wood Johnson Foundation)

www.finalthoughts.com (designed to assist people considering a wide range of end of life questions)

www.hospicecompassus.com (a rich resource which includes stories of patients and their families)

www.lastacts.org (caring at the end of life)

www.npr.org/programs/death (The End of Life. Exploring Death in America)

www.soros.org/death/index.htm (Project on Death in America)

Journals, Periodicals, Magazines

Archives of the Foundation of Thanatology. Vol. 1, 1969- . New York: Columbia College of Physicians and Surgeons.

Dickinson, George and Michael Leming, eds. *Annual Editions: Dying, Death and Bereavement.* New York: McGraw-Hill/ Duskin, 1997-

The Journal of Medicine and Philosophy, Vol 3, No. 1 (March 1978). issue on "Nature of Death".

Motive. January-February, 1964. Issue devoted to death. Of special value is the article, "The Day My Father Died," by Joseph Matthews.

Omega. An international journal for the psychological study of dying, death, bereavement, suicide and other lethal behaviors. Vol. 1, 1970- . Greenwood Publications.

Zygon: Journal of Religion and Science. Vol. 1, No. 4 (December 1966) Chicago.issue on "The Meaning of Death in the Evolution of Life"

General Works

Choron, Jacques. *Death and Western Thought.* New York: Macmillan, 1963.

Cutler, Donald R., ed. *Updating Life and Death: How to Face the Inevitable with Wisdom and Dignity.* Boston: Beacon Press, 1971.

Greinacher, Robert and Alois Miller. *The Experience of Dying.* New York: Herder and Herder, 1975.

Hendin, David. *Death as a Fact of Life.* New York: Norton, 1973.

Hinton, John. *Dying.* Baltimore: Penguin, 1967.

Johnston, Mark. *Surviving Death.* Princeton: Princeton University Press, 2010.

Jungel, Eberhard. *Death: the Riddle and the Mystery.* Philadelphia: Westminster, 1975.

Kastenbaum, Robert, ed. *Macmillan Encyclopedia of Death and Dying.*Detroit: Gale, 2002. 2 vols.

Lifton, Robert J. and Eric Olson. *And a Time to Die: Death and the Continuity of Life.* New York: Praeger, 1974.

Matousek, Mark, "The Last Taboo," *Modern Maturity* (September-October 2000), pp. 48-59.

Shields, David. *The thing About Life is that One Day You'll be Dead.* Reprint ed. New York: Vintage, 2009.

Smith, Rodney. *Lessons from the Dying.* Somerville, MA: Wisdom Publications, 1998.

Younger, Stuart J., Robert M. Arnold, and Renie Schapiro, eds. *The Definition of Death: Contemporary Controversies.* Baltimore: The Johns Hopkins University Press, 1999.

Anthropological, cultural (including American culture), ethnic and historical

Alaton, Salem, "Death at the boomer's party," *The Globe and Mail* (Canada) (May 18, 1996). p. D1-2.

Anderson, Patricia, ed. *All of Us: Americans Talk About the Meaning of Death.* New York: Delacorte,1996.

Aries, Philippe. *Western Attitudes Toward Death from the Middle Ages to the Present.* Baltimore: The Johns Hopkins University Press, 1974.

Barley, Nigel. *Grave Matters: a Lively History of Death around the World.* New York: Henry Holt, 1997.

Brink, Susan, "The American way of dying," *U.S. News & World Report,* (December 4, 1995) pp. 70-75.

Caarse, James P. *Death and Existence: A Conceptual History of Human Mortality.* New York: John Wiley, 1980.

Fontana, Andrea and Jennifer Reid Keene. *Death and Dying in America.* New York: John Wiley, 2009.

Frazer, James George. *The Belief in Immortality and the Worship of the Dead.* New York: Macmillan, 1913.

Frazer, James George. *Fear of the Dead in Primitive Religion.* Manchester, NH: Ayer Company Publication, 1933.

Irish, Donald P. and Kathleen F. Lundquist, eds. *Ethnic Variations in Dying, Death, and Grief: Diversity in Universality.* London: Taylor and Francis, 1993.

Miller, Lisa, "Living Well: Dying Well," *The Wall Street Journal* (February 25, 2000) pp. A1,A6.

Spiro, Howard, Lee Palmer Wendel, and Mary G. McCrea Cumen, eds. *Facing Death: Where Culture, Religion and Medicine Meet.* New Haven: Yale University Press, 1998.

Stannard, David E. *Death in America.* Philadelphia, PA: University of Pennsylvania Press, 1975.

Webb, Marilyn. *The Good Death: the new American search to reshape the end of life.* New York: Bantam Books, 1997.

Bereavement and Grief

Arnold, Joan Hagan and Penelope Buschman Gemma. *A Child Dies: A portrait of family grief.* 2nd ed. Philadelphia, PA: Charles Press, 1994.

Claypool, John. *Tracks of a Fellow Traveler: Learning How to Handle Grief.* Waco, TX: Word Books, 1974.

Frigo, Victoria and others. *You Can Help Someone Who's Grieving. A How to Healing Handbook.* Baltimore: Penguin, 1996.

Gordon, Jack D. and Kenneth J. Doka, eds. *Living with Grief: Children, Adolescents, and Loss.* Washington, DC: Hospice Foundation of America, 2000.

Gorer, Geoffrey. *Death, Grief, and Mourning.* New York: Doubleday, 1965.

Grollman, Earl A. *Talking About Death: a Dialogue Between Parent and Child.* Boston: Beacon, 1970.

Hafer, W. Keith. *Coping with Bereavement from Death and Divorce.* Upper Saddle River, NJ: Prentice Hall, 1999.

Jackson, Edgar. N. *Understanding Grief: its Roots, Dynamics, and Treatment.* Nashville: Abingdon, 1957.

Johnson, Janis, "Grief Doesn't Become Any Easier as we Grow Up," *USA Today* (May 4, 1983). p. 6D

Konigsberg, Ruth Davis. *The Truth About Grief,* New York: Simon & Schuster, 2011.

Krementz, Jill. *How It Feels When a Parent Dies.* New York: Knopf/Pantheon. 1988.

Lewis, C.S. *A Grief Observed.* Greenwich, CT: Seabury Press, 1963.

Myers, Edward. *When Parents Die: A Guide for Adults.* Rev. Ed. Baltimore: Penguin, 1997.

Roach, Sally and Beatriz Nieto. *Healing and the Grief Process.* Washington, DC: Thomson Delmar Learning, 1997.

Sanders, Catherine M. *Grief: The Mourning After: Dealing with Adult Bereavement.* 2nd ed. New York: John Wiley, 1999.

Tengbom, Mildred. *Help for Bereaved Parents.* St. Louis: Concordia, 1981.

Care for the dying/terminally ill; palliative care; hospice care

Beresford, Larry and Elisabeth Kubler-Ross. *The Hospice Handbook: a Complete Guide.* Boston: Little Brown, 1993.

Capposela, Cappy and Sheila Warnock. *Share the Care: How to organize a group to care for someone who is seriously ill.* Lady Lake, FL: Fireside, 1995.

Cassel, Christine K. and Marilyn J. Fields, eds. *Approaching Death: Improving care at the end of life.* Atlanta, GA: National Academy Press, 1997.

Connor, Stephen R. *Hospice and Palliative Care: The Essential Guide.* 2nd ed. London: Routledge, 2009

Conte, Christopher, "A Troubling Death," *AARP Bulletin* (January 1996) pp. 4-6.

Dobihal, Edward F., Jr. and Charles William Stewart. *When a Friend is Dying: A Guide to Caring for the Terminally Ill and Bereaved.* Nashville: Abingdon, 1984.

Doka, Kenneth J. *Living with Life-threatening Illness: A guide for patients, their families, and caregivers.* San Francisco: Jossey-Bass, 1998.

Fine, P.G. *The Hospice Companion.* Oxford: Oxford University Press, 2008.

Glasheen, Leah K. "Humanizing end-of-life care" *AARP Bulletin* (June 1997) pp. 2, 11-12

Glasheen, Leah K. and Susan L. Crowley, "A Family affair: Hospice eases the way at life's end," *AARP Bulletin* (May 1998) pp. 2, 10-12.

Glaven, Denise, Cindy Longanacre, and John Spivey. *Hospice: A Labor of Love.* St. Louis: Chalice Press, 1999.

Lamerton, Richard. *Care of the Dying.* New York: Penguin, 1981

Lynn, Joanne and Joan Harrold. *Handbook for Mortals: Guidance for people facing serious illness.* Oxford: Oxford University Press, 1999.

Meyer, Charles. *A Good Death: Challenges, choices and care options.* New London, CT: Twenty Third Publications, 1998.

Meyer, Maria and Paula Derr. *The Comfort of Home: An illustrated step-by-step guide for caregivers.* Portland, OR: CareTrust Publications, 1998.

Olson, Melodie. *Healing the Dying.* Washington, DC: Thomson Delmar Learning, 1997.

Quill, Timothy E. *A Midwife through the Dying Process: Stories of Healing and Hard Choices at the End of Life.* Baltimore: Johns Hopkins University Press, 1996.

Saunders, Cicely. *Care of the Dying.* New York: Macmillan, 1959.

Saunders, Cicely. *Hospice: The Living Idea.* London: Hodder Arnold, 1981.

Sendor, Virginia F. and Patrice M. O'Connor. *Hospice and Palliative Care: Questions and Answers.* Lanham, MD: Scarecrow Press, 1997.

Tobin, Dan. *Peaceful Dying.* New York: Perseus Books, 1998.

Caring for the dying and comforting the living; funerals, ministry

Baker, Beth, "Fighting for funeral rights," *AARP Bulletin* (November 1999) pp. 18-20.

Bennett, Amanda and Terence B. Foley. *In Memoriam: a practical guide to planning a memorial service.* New York: Simon and Shuster, 1997.

"Funeral franchise? Death is big business," *The Sun* (Kitsap County, WA) (November 23, 1995) p. G2.

Lessem, Jeanne, "They'll get you in the end: Hard-sell marketing practices," *The Blade-Tribune* (Oceanside, CA) (November 1, 1978) p. 32.

Lynch, Thomas. *The Undertaking: Life studies from the dismal trade.* New York: Norton, 1997.

Marshall, George N. *Facing Death and Grief.* New York: Prometheus Books, 1981.

Van Tuyl, Joyce. *What You Should Know About Death Services.* Seattle: People's Memorial Association, 1991.

Wolfelt, Alan. *Death and Grief: A Guide for Clergy.* London: Accelerated Development, 1988.

Coping with death and dying; death education

Bailey, Rex, "Students at Transylvania are learning about death," *The Courier-Journal* (Louisville) (December 16, 1974) p. B-1

Balk, David, ed. *Handbook of Thanatology: The Essential Body of Knowledge for the Study of Death, Dying, and Bereavement.* London: Routledge, 2007.

Bastian, Edward and others, eds. *Living Fully, Dying Well: Reflecting on Death to Find Your Life's Meaning.* Louisville, CO: Sounds True, 2009.

Bertman, Sandra L. *Facing Death: Images, Insights, and Interventions: A Handbook for Educators, Healthcare Professionals, and Counselors.* London: Taylor and Francis, 1991

Biegert, John E. *My Loved One is Dying.* Rev. ed. Boston: Pilgrim, 2004

Caine, Lynn. *Widows.* New York: William Morrow, 1974.

Corr, Charles A., Clyde M. Nabe, and Donna M. Corr. *Death and Dying: Life and Living.* 6th ed. Belmont, CA: Wadsworth, 2008.

Grollman, Earl A. *When Your Loved One is Dying.* Boston: Beacon Press, 1980.

Halifax, Joan and Ira Byock. *Being with Dying: Cultivating Compassion and Fearlessness in the Presence of Death.* Boston, MA: Shambhala, 2008.

Kessler, David. *The Needs of the Dying: A Guide for Bringing Hope, Comfort, and Love to Life's Final Chapter.* 10th Anniversary ed. New York: Harper, 2007.

Maddocks, Melvin, "Death's a Finale, so make it Good," *The National Observer.* (February 15, 1975) p. 22.

Malino, J.R., "Coping with Death in Western Religious Civilization," *Zygon: Journal of Religion and Science.* Vol. I, No. 4 (December 1966) pp. 354-365.

Noel, Brook and Pamela D. Blair. *I Wasn't Ready to say Goodbye: Surviving, Coping, and Healing After the Sudden Death of a Loved One.* Naperville, IL: Sourcebooks, 2008.

Nye, Miriam Baker. *But I Never Thought He'd Die: Practical Help for Widows.* Philadelphia: Westminster, 1978.

Schaefer, Dan and Christine Lyons. *How do we Tell the Children? A step-by-step guide for helping children two to teen cope when someone dies.* New York: Newmarket Press, 1993.

Ethical issues in death and dying

Barnard, Christian. *Good Life/Good Death: A Doctor's Case for Euthanasia and Suicide.* Upper Saddle River, NJ: Prentice Hall, 1980.

Beauchamp Tom L. and Seymour Perlin, eds. *Ethical Issues in Death and Dying.* Upper Saddle River, NJ: Prentice-Hall, 1987.

Foley, Kathleen and Herbert Hendin, eds. *The Case Against Assisted Suicide: For the Right to End-of-Life Care.* Baltimore: Johns Hopkins University Press, 2002.

High, Dallas M. *Medical Treatment of the Dying: Moral Issues.* Lexington, KY: University of Kentucky Press,1978.

Koop, C. Everett. *Right to Live: Right to Die.* Carol Stream, IL: Tyndale Press, 1976.

Ladd, John. *Ethical Issues Relating to Life and Death.* Oxford: Oxford University Press, 1979.

Maguire, Daniel C. *Death by Choice.* New York: Doubleday, 1974.

Mannes, Marya. *Last Rights: A Case for the Good Death.* New York: William Morrow, 1974.

Nelson, James B. *Human Medicine: Ethical Perspectives on Medical Issues.* Milwaukee, WI: Augsburg, 1973.

Ramsey, Paul. *The Patient as Person: Explorations in Medical Ethics.* New Haven: Yale University Press, 1970.

Vaux, Kenneth, ed. *Who Shall Live?* Philadelphia, PA: Fortress Press, 1970.

Veatch, Robert M. *Death, Dying, and the Biological Revolution: Our Last Quest for Responsibility.* New Haven: Yale University Press, 1965,

Vischer, M.B., ed. *Humanistic Perspectives in Medical Ethics.* New York: Prometheus Books, 1972.

Wilson, Jerry B. *Death by Decision: the medical, moral, and legal dilemmas of euthanasia.* Philadelphia: Westminster, 1975.

Literary treatments of death and dying

Agee, James. *A Death in the Family.* New York: Avon,1957.

Baer, Lydia. *Concept and Function of Death in Writings of Thomas Mann.* Philadelphia, PA: University of Pennsylvania Press, 1931.

Benedictus, David. *Whose Life is it Anyway?* West Sussex: Littlehampton Book Services, 1982. novel adapted from Brian Clark's play of the same name.

Bierce, Ambrose, "An Occurance at Owl Creek Bridge,"

Cather, Willa, "Neighbour Rosicky"

Davidson, David. *The Steeper Cliff.* New York: Random House, 1947.

DeVries, Peter, *The Blood of the Lamb.* Chicago: University of Chicago Press, 2005.

Eliot, T.S. *Murder in the Cathedral.* New York: Harcourt, Brace, 1935.

Fiedler, Leslie A. *Love and Death in the American Novel.* London: Secker and Warburg, 1961.

Ford, T.W. *Heaven Beguiles the Tired: Death in the Poetry of Emily Dickinson* Tuscaloosa, AL:. University of Alabama Press, 1968.

Frost, Robert, "*Death of the Hired Man,*" 1914.

Heller, Joseph J. *Catch 22.* New York: Dell, 1970.

Hemingway, Ernest. *Death in the Afternoon.* New York: Halcyon House,1932.

Hoffman, Frederick John. *The Mortal No: Death and the Modern Imagination.* Princeton: Princeton University Press, 1964.

Koestler, Arthur. *Dialogue with Death.* Trs. Trevor and Phyllis Blewitt, New York: Macmillan, 1960.

Kurtz, Benjamin P. *The Pursuit of Death: A Study of Shelley's Poetry.* London: Octagon, 1933.

Maeterlinck, Maurice. *Death.* Tr, Alexander Teixeira de Mattos. Indianapolis, IN: Dodd, Mead, 1912.

Miller, Alexander. "A Reflection on Some Attitudes Toward Death in Contemporary Non-Christian Writing," *Encounter,* Vol. XXII (Winter 1961) pp. 84-91.

Miller, Arthur. *Death of a Salesman.* New York: Viking, 1966.

Porter, Katherine Anne, "The Jilting of Granny Weatherall,"

Rose, William. "Rilke and the Conception of Death," *Rainer Maria Rilke: Aspects of His Mind and Poetry.* William Rose and C. Craig Houston, eds. with an introduction by Stephan Qweig. London: Sidgwick and Jackson, 1938. pp. 41-84.

Salinas, Pedro, "Lorca and the Poetry of Death." *The Hopkins Review,* Vol. V, (Fall 1951) pp. 5-12.

Sayers, Dorothy. *The Zeal of Thy House.* London: Victor Gollanez, 1937.

Serling, Rod, "Stop at Willoughby," and "They're Tearing Down Tim Riley's Bar"

Slater, Scott and Alec Solomita. *Exits: Dying Words and Last Moments.* Boston: Dutton, 1980.

Solzhenitsyn, Alexander. *Cancer Ward.* Farrar, New York: Straus & Giroux, 1991.

Weir, Robert F., ed. *Death in Literature.* New York: Columbia University Press, 1980.

Whitman, Walt, "The Passage to India" and "Death Carol"

Wilder, Thornton, "Our Town"

Medical treatments of death

Ackerknecht, E.H., "Death in the History of Medicine," *Bulletin of the History of Medicine.* Vol. 42, 1968. pp.19-23.

Baer, L.S. *Let the Patient Decide: A Doctor's Advice to Older Persons.* Philadelphia: Westminster, 1978.

Bercu, Barry B., Allen W. Root, Dorothy I. Shulman, "The Dying Patient, the physician, and the fear of death," *The New England Journal of Medicine,* Vol. 319, No. 26 (December 29, 1988) pp.1728-1730.

Browne, Thomas. *Religio Medici.* A new edition with biographical and critical introduction by Jean-Jacques Denonain. Cambridge University Press, 1955.

Halley, M. Martin and William F. Harvey, "Medical vs. Legal Definitions of Death," *Journal of the American Medical Association.* Vol. 204, No. 6 (May 6, 1968) pp. 423-425.

Jaroff, Leon, "Knowing When to Stop" *Time Magazine* (December 4, 1995) p. 76.

Lasagna, Louis, "The Doctor and the dying patient," *Journal of Chronic Diseases.* Vol. 2, No. 2, 1969. pp. 65-68.

Mack, Robert M., "Making Life Count," *The Seattle Times* (January 20, 1985) pp. K1, K5, K6.

Morrison, Robert S., "Death, Process or Event?" *Science,* Vol. 173 (August 20, 1971) pp. 694-698.

Saunders, Ciceley, "The Last Stages of Life," *American Journal of Nursing.* Vol. 65 (March 1965) pp. 70-75.

Schnaper, Nathan. "Death and Dying: Has the Topic Been Beaten to Death?" *The Journal of Nervous and Mental Disease.* Vol. 160, No. 3 (March 1975) pp. 157-158.

Seravalli, Egilde P., "The Dying Patient, The Physician, and the Fear of Death," *The New England Journal of Medicine* (December 29, 1988) pp.1728-1730.

Personal memoirs and reflections

Alsop, Stewart. *Stay of Execution: a sort of Memoir.* New York: Lippincott, 1973.

Cohen, Richard. "She Chose to Die at Home with Chris," *Los Angeles Times,* (November 22, 1979) p. 10. part VIII of a series.

Derksen, Sandy and Connie Nash. *The Other Side of Sorrow.* Milwaukee, WI: Augsburg, 1982.

Gandhi: An Autobiography, The Story of My Experiments with Truth. Boston: Beacon Press, 1993. Ch. IX: "My Father's Death and My Double Shame,"

Graham, Jory, "An Instant Death Cheats the Family," *Independent, Press-Telegram* (Long Beach, CA) (December 7, 1980) pp. L/S3.

Gunther, John. *Death Be Not Proud: A Memoir.* New York: Perennial, 1949.

Johnson, Margaret Woods. *We Lived with Dying.* Waco, TX: Word Books, 1975.

MacPherson, Myra. *She Came to Live Out Loud: An inspiring family journey through illness, loss, and grief.* New York: Scribner, 1999.

Remen, Rachael Naomi. *My Grandfather's Blessings.* New York: Riverhead Books, 2000.

Sittser, Gerald L. *A Grace Disguised: How the soul grows through loss.* Grand Rapids, MI: Zondervan, 1996.

Thomas, Pat. *I Miss You: A First Look at Death.* New York: Barron's Educational Series, 2001.

Wertenbaker, Lael Tucker. *Death of A Man.* New York: Random House, 1957.

Zickgraf, Cordula. *I am Learning to Live Because you Must Die: A Hospital Diary.* Milwaukee, WI: Fortress, 1981.

Philosophical treatments of death

Boros, Ladislaus. *The Mystery of Death.* Greenwich, Ct: Seabury Press, 1973.

DeBeauvoir, Simone. *A Very Easy Death.* New York: Putnams, 1966.

Demske, James M. *Being, Man, and Death.* Lexington: University of Kentucky Press, 1970.

Flew, Anthony, ed. *Body, Mind and Death*. New York: Macmillan, 1964.

High, Dallas M., "Death: its Conceptual Elusiveness," *Soundings*. Vol. 55 (Winter 1972) pp. 438-458.

Hope, Richard, "Plato's *Phaedo* on Deathlessness," *The Personalist*, Vol. XXXII, No. 1 (January 1951) pp. 19-25.

Kaufmann, Walter, "Existentialism and Death," *The Meaning of Death*. Herman Feifel, ed. New York: McGraw Hill, 1959. pp. 39-63.

Kierkegaard Soren A. *The Sickness Unto Death*. Tr. Walter Lowrie. Princeton: Princeton University Press, 1941.

Marcuse, Herbert, "The Ideology of Death," *The Meaning of Death*. Herman Feifel, ed. New York: McGraw Hill, 1959. pp. 64-76.

Marks, Elaine. *Simone de Beauvoir: Encounters with Death*. Rutgers, NJ: Rutgers University Press, 1973.

Unamuno, Miguel de *The Tragic Sense of Life*. Tr. J.E, Crawford Flitch. New York: Dover Publications, 1954.

Whitehead, Alfred North, "Immortality," *The Harvard Divinity School Bulletin*, 1942. pp. 5-20.

Psychological treatments of death

Becker, Ernest. *The Denial of Death*. Glencoe, IL: Free Press, 1974.

Berman, Eric. *Scapegoat: The Impact of Death Fear on an American Family*. Ann Arbor: University of Michigan Press, 1973.

Brown, Norman O. *Life Against Death*. New York: Random House, 1959.

Eissler, Kurt R. *The Psychiatrist and the Dying Patient*. New York: International Universities Press,1955.

Frankl, Viktor Emil. *Man's Search for Meaning*. New York: Washington Square Press, 1959. Earlier published as *The Doctor and the Soul: An Introduction to Logotherapy*. Tr. Richard and Clara Winston. New York: Alfred A. Knopf, 1955.

Glaser, Barney G. *Time for Dying.* Chicago: Aldine, 1969.

Koestenbaum, Peter. *Vitality of Death: Essays in Existential Psychology and Philosophy.* Oxford: Greenwood, 1971.

Leming, Michael K. and George E. Dickinson. *Understanding Dying, Death and Bereavement.* 6th ed. Belmont, CA: Wadsworth, 2006.

Schneidman, Edwin S., ed. *Death: Current Perspectives.* 2nd ed. Palo Alto, CA: Mayfield, 1980.

Sudnow, D. *Passing On.* Upper Saddle River, NJ: Prentice Hall, 1967.

Tarnower, W., "The dying patient: psychological needs of the patient, his family, and the physician," *Nebraska Medical Journal.* Vol. 54 (anuary 1969) pp. 6-10.

Wyschogrod, Edith, ed. *The Phenomenon of Death: faces of mortality.* New York: Harper & Row, 1973.

Religious treatments of death

Badham, Paul and Linda Badham. *Death and Immortality in the Religions of the World.* New York: Paragon House, 1987.

Bailey, Lloyd R. Sr. *Biblical Perspectives on Death (Overtures to Biblical Theology, 4).* Philadelphia: Fortress Press, 1979.

Baillie, John. *And the Life Everlasting.* New York: Charles Scribner's Sons, 1933.

Dicks, Russell.L. and Thomas S. Kepler. *And Peace at the Last: a study of Death, the Unreconciled Subject of our Times.* Philadelphia: Westminster, 1953.

Eliade, Mircea. *Death, Afterlife, and Eschatology.* New York: Harper, 1974.

Graham, Billy. *Facing Death and the Life After.* Nashville, TN: W. Publishing Group, 1987.

Holck, Frederick H., ed. *Death and Eastern Thought: Understanding Death in Eastern Religions and Philosophies.* Nashville: Abingdon, 1976.

Kramer, Kenneth. *The Sacred Art of Dying: How the World Religions Understand Death.* New York: Paulist Press, 1988.

Lee, Jung Young. *Death and Beyond in the Eastern Perspective.* Interface/Gordon and Breach, 1974.

Lund, Sharon. *Sacred Living, Sacred Dying: A Guide to Embracing Life and Death.* New York: iUniverse, 2006.

McLemore, Bonnie. *Death, Sin and the Moral Life: Contemporary Cultural Interpretations of Death.* Atlanta, GA: Scholars Press, 1988.

Riemer, Jack. *Jewish Reflections on Death.* New York: Schocken, 1974.

Rosen, Steven J. *Ultimate Journey: Death and Dying in the World's Major Religions.* New York: Praeger, 2008.

Sellers, James E. *When Trouble Comes.* Nashville: Abingdon, 1960.

Shinn, Roger Lincoln. *Life, Death, and Destiny.* Philadelphia: Westminster, 1957.

Smart, Ninian, "Attitudes towards Death in Eastern Religions," in *Man's Concern with Death.* Arnold Toynbee and others, eds. New York: McGraw Hill, 1969. pp.95-115.

Stendahl, Krister, ed. *Immortality and Resurrection.* New York: Macmillan, 1965.

Taylor. A. E. *The Christian Hope of Immortality.* London: Unicorn Press, 1938.

About the Author

Paul Warren Murphey has taught college and adult education courses and workshops on death and dying for fifty years. His doctoral dissertation was titled: *The Problem of Death in the Theology of Nicholas Berdyaev, Paul Tillich, and Helmut Thielicke.*

He grew up in Augusta, GA where he was active in Central Christian Church. He was ordained to the Christian ministry at Woodmont Christian Church, Nashville, TN. He and his wife are members of Summit Avenue Presbyterian Church, Bremerton, WA.

He was College Chaplain and taught history, philosophy, religion, and sociology at Eureka College, Illinois. He was then Professor of Religion and Director of the Interdisciplinary Humanities Program at Transylvania University, Lexington, Kentucky. He has taught as an adjunct faculty member at Bradley University, the University of Kentucky, Chapman University (Bangor Campus), City University of Seattle, Seattle Pacific University and Olympic College.

While teaching at Transylvania he served as a Naval Reserve Chaplain. He left college teaching to go on active duty serving in both sea and shore billets on the West Coast and in Japan. After retiring he returned to Bremerton, WA where he resumed college teaching on a part-time basis. Almost 20 years ago he became deeply involved in the work of Hospice of Kitsap County serving as President of the Board of Trustees and as a respite care giver. He has been active in the Community through church involvement in teaching adult classes as well as in the Rotary Club of Silverdale.

His Ph.D. was granted by Vanderbilt University. He also holds a M.Div degree from Vanderbilt Divinity School; an MSLS degree from the University of Kentucky, an MBA degree from City University of Seattle. His BA degree is from Texas Christian University.

He has four grown children, seven grandchildren, and two great grandchildren.

He has been a member of several professional organizations throughout his career and is currently a member of the American Philosophical Association, the Association of Practical and Professional Ethics, and the Society of Christian Ethics.

He is listed in *Who's Who in America,* 2012 and may be contacted via email at pwmurphey@wavecable.com, by telephone at 360-930-4120 or mail at 12163 Country Meadows LN NW #201, Silverdale, WA 98383.